What You Should Know About **Anti-Corruption**

Dr. Reem Ali Al-Anssari

Hamad Bin Khalifa University Press
P.O. Box 5825
Doha, Qatar

www.hbkupress.com

First English edition in 2022

ISBN: 9789927155642

Printed in Doha-Qatar

Qatar National Library Cataloging-in-Publication (CIP)

Al-Anssari, Reem Ali, author.

What you should know about anti-corruption / Dr. Reem Ali Al-Anssari. – First English edition. - Doha, Qatar : Hamad Bin Khalifa University Press, 2022.

pages ; cm. – (Simply said series)

ISBN 978-992-715-564-2

Includes bibliographical references.

1. Corruption -- Law and legislation. 2. Corruption -- History. 3. Corruption -- Prevention. I. Title.

K5261 .A957 2022
345.02323– dc 23 202228321583

Contents

INTRODUCTION

Teaching anti-corruption in educational institutions is something new. It is uncommon – almost a taboo – to find people using the word corruption itself, although they may refer to examples of it, in their efforts to raise awareness of corruption in different sectors of society.

This book is the distillation of real-life experiences in classrooms, lecture halls, consortiums and conferences, which involved students, experts in the field, non-experts, professionals, peers and family members as well. It will offer a clear framework which anyone can relate to, simplifying the complicated legalese.

The aim of this book is to describe the fields of corruption and anti-corruption. It is the decision of readers how they will conceptualize what they learn from their reading, what they do with it and where it takes them. Hopefully they will learn how to reason organically until they arrive at their own unique conclusions.

The book is arranged as follows. Chapter one offers a theoretical framework and discusses the origins of anti-corruption. Chapter two focuses on ways of preventing and dealing with it, describing the legal framework, legal instruments, case examples, investigative and competent authorities. Chapter three outlines the United Nations Convention Against Corruption and its importance. Chapters four, five and six offer in-depth, real life examples of anti-corruption in the fields of education, healthcare, and in the humanitarian sector. Finally, the last section presents conclusions and suggests the way forward.

CHAPTER ONE:
WHAT IS CORRUPTION?

1.1 ORIGINS OF CORRUPTION

There is a well-known saying: "If it stings, it upsets you!". We are not all exposed to the same level of corruption, but even if one is not suffering directly from it, it is better to be prepared before it stings. And even if there is no chance of it stinging, at least one should acquire the necessary skills to help others understand, deal with and overcome it.

In order to understand something, you must know where it came from. What is the origin of the term "corruption"? What does it look like? To answer these questions, it goes without saying that corruption has always been deeply rooted in the social, historical and political structure of states.[1] It is as old as human history, and it mutates.

Any attempt to analyze the concept of corruption must contend with the fact that even in international languages such as English and Arabic, the word "corruption" has a history of vastly different meanings and connotations[2] and the nuances do not allow a single historical conclusion. Its meaning continues to evolve even as these

---

1 Daron Acemoglu & James A. Robinson, *Why Nations Fail: The Origins of Power, Prosperity and Poverty*, 29 Asian Econ. Bul. 168 (2012).

2 Arnold Joseph Heidenheimer & Michael Johnston, Political Corruption, Concepts and Contexts (2009).

words are written. However, a discussion of the theoretical and historical perspectives of corruption as shown in its different forms over time sheds some light on what it means in reality.

> *Just as fish moving underwater cannot possibly be found out either as drinking or not drinking water, so government servants employed in government work cannot be found out (while) taking money (for themselves).*[1]

These words were penned by the philosopher Kautilya, also known as Chanakya or Vishnugupta, in his treatise known as the *Arthashastra*, which was written in India and dates back to the fourth century B.C. In a passage of remarkable and characteristic precision in this treatise, Kautilya states that there are "forty ways of embezzlement" and goes on to enumerate them. Clearly, corruption is a complex problem as well as an ancient one.[2] As Kautilya shows, corruption in one form or another has always been with us. It is a phenomenon that permeates every social structure, with consequences that are difficult to measure in economic terms. However, it is far from uniform. It has had variegated appearances at different times and in different places. As mentioned previously, it has mutated, with varying degrees of damaging consequences. While the tenacity with which it persists in some cases leads to despair and resignation on the part of its combatants, a whole range of policy measures can and have helped to assuage the effects of corruption.

The concept of corruption will be explored from the secular derivatives of human antiquity, particularly in Babylonian, Egyptian, Chinese, Greek and Roman cultures as well as from religious/non-secular derivatives by exploring divinely-inspired texts that contribute to the definition. Religion impacts many human beings

---

1 The Kautilya Arthasastra, Part II (R.P. Kangle ed., 1972).

2 Pranab Bardhan, *Corruption and Development: A Review of Issues* 35 J. Econ. Lit. 1320 (1997).

and different faiths speak about the origin of corruption in different terms. Therefore, the chapter also examines the religious texts of Judaism, Christianity and Islam. The result is a deeper understanding of corruption, its effect on society and where this ancient concept may be headed.

FIGURE 1

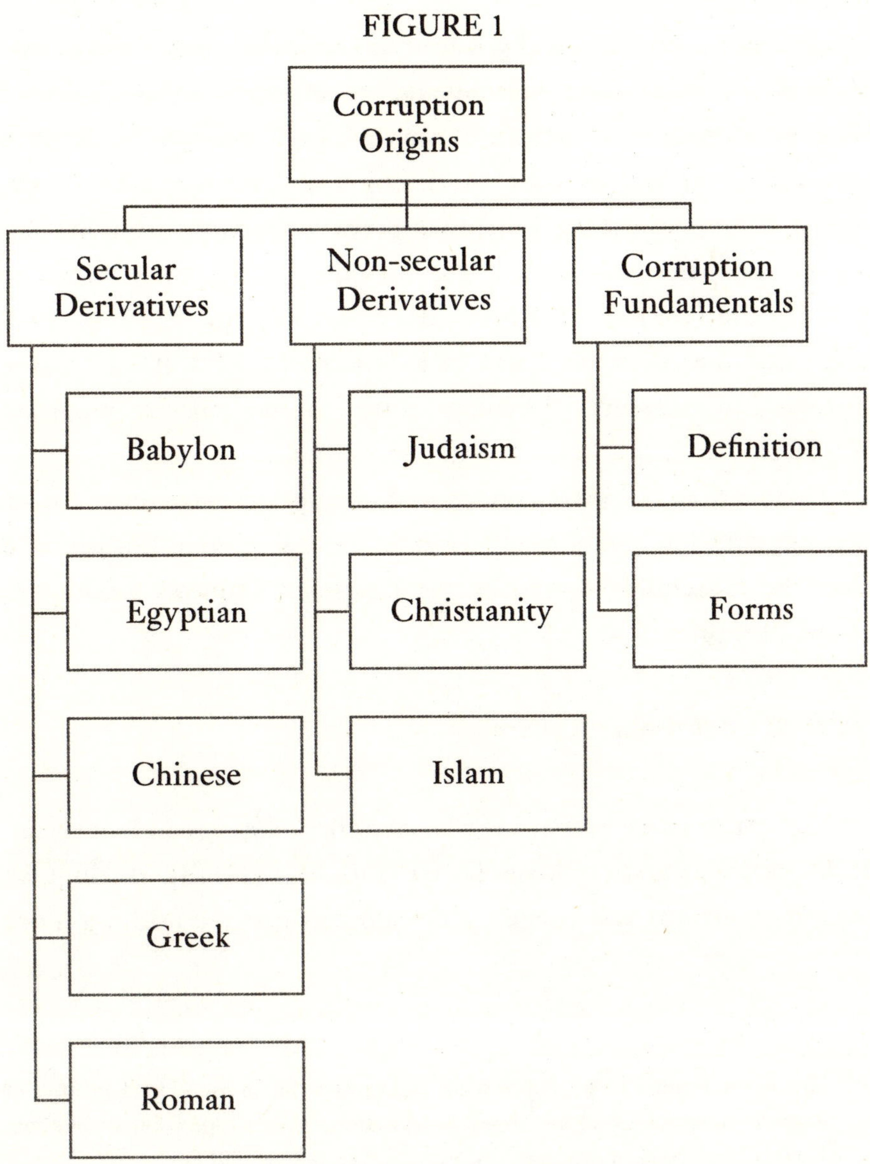

1.2 SECULAR DERIVATIVES

An interest in justice and awareness of the negative effects of administrative, political and social wrongdoing is evident from the very beginnings of civilization itself. Once nomadic tribal peoples began to settle in permanent organized societies, they began to create rules to regulate and govern their behavior that might enable them to avoid complete anarchy and the arbitrary abuse of power.[1] The development of writing permitted such rules to be written down and recorded as laws.[2] Archaeologists have discovered fragments of the earliest legal documents and collections from ancient Egypt and Mesopotamia.[3] These include the Sumerian Code of Ur-Nammu (c. 2100-2050 B.C.), the codex of Lipit-Ishtar (c. 1930 B.C.) and the Akkadian Laws of Eshnunna (c. 1770 B.C.).[4] These historical documents illuminate some of the earliest recorded instances of corruption in ancient governments.

This section will give examples of corruption from several eras, starting with the cradle of civilization, the Babylonian Empire, and then the subsequent dynasties: the Egyptian, Chinese, Greek and Roman Empires.

1.2.1 The Babylonian Empire

A bright thread runs between corruption, offerings and sacrifices. It bears investigation because we should naturally distinguish between customs and usages, although this may be nothing more

---

1 *Id.*

2 *Id.*

3 *Id.*

4 The most detailed treatment of these legal codes can be found in A History of Ancient Near Eastern Law (Raymond Westbrook ed., 2003); Dinah Shelton, Oxford Handbook of International Human Rights Law (2013).

than a mere matter of nuance.[1] In this sense, the ancient Babylonian empire represents the main reference for understanding the concept of corruption as it relates to customs. The types of symbolic scheme that dominated political and economic decisions of the time and the methods of exchange used by some of the parties involved show this connection.[2]

In the age of the Sumerians and Semites, King Urukagina (or Uruinimghina) of Lagash, the ancient city-state of Sumer, reorganized the state administration in order to put an end to the abuses of its officials and judges. He regulated payments for ceremonies and stood against the corruption and greed of the clergy, accusing them of avarice for taking bribes in administering the law and for oppressing farmers and fishermen. These measures rid the administration of corrupt officials, establishing laws that regulated the taxes paid to the temples and protecting King Urukagina's people against extortion.[3]

After the kings of Sumer and Akkad (Sumer was the south and Akkad the north of the region of Lower Mesopotamia, two great divisions which made up Babylon in that period), the rulers struggled to maintain order in Mesopotamia, and the old Babylonian empire emerged.[4] Forms of corruption were preserved by the existing systems within social classes, and written systems upheld corruption as *quid pro quo*.[5] In essence, a religious practice such as sacrifice constitutes, with all the distinctions and caveats that we might apply to a ritual and its attendant symbolisms, a form of *quid*

---

1 Carlo Alberto Brioschi, Corruption a Short Story: The Gift in Antiquity: Exchange Favor and Sacrifice from Hammurabi to the Bible 21-28 (2017).

2 *Id.*

3 W. Durant, The Story of Civilization: Part I - Our Oriental Heritage (1935).

4 Leonard W. King, A History of Sumer and Akkad (1994).

5 Jack Newton Lawson, The Concept of Fate in Ancient Mesopotamia of the First Millennium: Towards an Understanding of Šīmtu: Šīmtu and Humanity 76 (1994).

pro quo,[1] a Latin phrase meaning "something for something". It is an exchange of acts or things of approximately equal value.[2]

This concept of sacrifice as *quid pro quo* is also known as the "law of reciprocity" and there are other illustrations of it in Hammurabi's code.[3] According to this code, corruption appears through "bending the bond of reciprocity" as phrased by American judge John Thomas Noonan in his book entitled *Bribes*.[4] It happens when there is a failure to offer equal value in exchange for value received, which in turn defies the logic of exchange and constitutes a violation of the concept.[5]

Most of Hammurabi's English editors entitle this section of the laws of Babylon "The Corrupt Judge".[6] There are a number of instances of such corruption in Hammurabi's legislation,[7] exemplified in the notion of "tatu".[8] This is when a judge delivers a decision and then changes his mind. He may be a judge who receives a bribe, gives the expected verdict, and then reneges. The word "tatu" used in the text of Hammurabi in this section generally indicates an offering made by a subordinate.[9]

---

1 Brioschi, *supra* note 9.

2 *Quid Pro Quo*, Legal Info. Inst., https://www.law.cornell.edu/wex/quid_pro_quo (last visited June 1, 2019).

3 Erwiin J. Urch, *The Law Code of Hammurabi*, 15 A.B.A. J. 437 (1929).

4 John Thomas Noonan, Bribes: The Intellectual History of an Idea Moral 2-7 (1987).

5 *Id.*

6 Nau Nihal Singh, World of Bribery and Corruption: From the Ancient Times to Modern Age 5-8 (1998).

7 Judges like Kushshiharbe, the mayor of Nuzi in northern Iraq who took "tatu"—which generically indicates the unreciprocated offering of a subordinate; the subordinate did not reciprocate. He went on trial for a variety of crimes and later denied them. Alexander Humez et al., Short Cuts: A Guide to Oaths, Ring Tones, Ransom Notes, Famous Last Words, and Other Forms of Minimalist Communication 209 (2010).

8 Brioschi, *supra* note 9.

9 *Id.*

According to historical texts, offerings and corruption merge one into the other, creating a grey area where "corruption" is often considered utterly normal and even preferred. A more generalized condemnation of corrupt giving would only arrive later, in the modern age. The notions of sacrifice and favor and the concept of corruption must be kept quite separate, particularly bearing in mind the historic and religious rules which are followed and revered by devotees.[1] From a secular and historical standpoint, an example of corruption appeared in the fact that Hammurabi's editors state that there were no instances of the Babylonian judge's being bribed, yet it occurred in the background. The custom of gift giving was widespread, and consequently it is hard to be sure that Hammurabi intended in his Code to prevent cases of the corruption of judges.[2] It is possible, instead, that the punishment mentioned had to do with verdicts not being applied, or even cases of judges who had not done their part in exchange for a gift.[3]

From a very different perspective to that of Hammurabi, Kautilya, the Brahmin of the fourth century B.C., wrote a fascinating book on the art of government entitled *Arthashastra*, quoted earlier at the beginning of this chapter. It is an important source on this topic. His treatise may be translated as "Instructions on Material Prosperity",[4] but the Indian economist Amartya Sen has suggested a simpler translation: "Economics". The Sanskrit text, discovered in 1905, explores the vast and evergreen phenomenon of corruption.[5] Although it was and still is difficult to prove dishonesty, since it does not have a material manifestation and resides within the heart and intention of human beings, yet, as per Kautilya's adages, those who

1 Baruch Ottervanger, The Tale of the Poor Man of Nippur (Penn. State Univ. 2016).

2 Brioschi, *supra* note 9.

3 *Id.*

4 *Id.*

5 *Id.*

govern use every means to achieve their objectives. Rules of rigor and honesty seem to apply,[1] at least in substance, only to their subjects.

Originally included in Noonan's aforementioned book *Bribes*, and updated by Baruch Ottervanger for the State Archives of Assyria Cuneiform Texts series, is "The Poor Man of Nippur",[2] an ancient folk tale transcribed by Olivier Robert Gurney.[3] This story, which revolves around the idea of *quid pro quo*, also known as "reciprocity", originates from about 1500 B.C. in ancient Mesopotamia.[4] Reciprocity was then strictly respected, since breaches in the logic of exchange led to punishment.[5] Therefore, the misdeed lay not in the act of making a gift, but rather in failing to offer value in exchange for the value received.

In *Bribes*, Noonan comments that the most serious misdeed lay not in the act of corrupting, but in the effect of corruption: breaking one's word in a society where keeping one's word was a divine characteristic.[6]

Of particular note is *The Tale of the Poor Man of Nippur*. This story is purely secular. No god is named or invoked, and the moral structure is supplied by the rule of reciprocity. The tale revolves around a poor man who, when wronged by the governor of Nippur, cunningly takes revenge on his abuser and wrongdoer. Gimil-Ninurta, the poor man, gives the mayor his goat in an attempt to improve his lot.[7] The mayor then announces that he will hold a

1 *Id.*

2 Ottervanger, *supra* note 23.

3 Wolfgang Saxon, *Oliver R. Gurney, 86, Professor and Expert on Ancient Hittites*, N.Y. Times (Jan. 27, 2001), https://www.nytimes.com/2001/01/27/world/oliver-r-gurney-86-professor-and-expert-on-ancient-hittites.html.

4 Noonan, *supra* note 17.

5 Brioschi, *supra* note 9.

6 *Id.*

7 Ottervanger, *supra* note 23.

feast,[1] but when the feast is held, all that Gimil-Ninurta receives is a bone and sinew of the goat. He asks the meaning of such treatment, but in reply, he is beaten on the mayor's orders. He departs, vowing retaliation. Gimil-Ninurta executes his revenge through activating the notion of reciprocity. He visits the king of Nippur and offers him a mina of gold in return for loan of his chariot for a day. Using the chariot, Gimil returns to Nippur and is received as a well-respected official at the mayor's residence. Gimil claims that an amount of gold in the chariot has disappeared. The mayor, lacking the temerity to defend himself, placates Gimil with a gift of two minas of gold.[2] Gimil-Ninurta returns triumphant in the royal chariot, unrecognized by the mayor as the man he had mistreated!

Here it can be seen that the misdeed lay not in the act of making a gift in one's own interest, but rather in the receiver failing to offer value in exchange for value received. Gimil expected something in return, yet the mayor defied the logic of reciprocity and became the villain when he took what was given and failed to reciprocate adequately. Furthermore, another implied form of corruption appears in the silence of the king against the background of the mayor's wrongdoing to Gimil. This, in and of itself, can be construed a form of unjust, corrupt behavior.

1.2.2 Egyptian Dynasties

At the time of the ancient Egyptian empire, corruption was linked to Pharaonic ritual. Due to a well-known Pharaonic belief in life after death, when the dead could interact with the living, Egyptian tombs were filled with furniture, clothes, jewelry, food and drink, and tomb robbing occurred. Criminals in the late Ramses period testified to everything from the theft of objects from tombs to

---

1 Noonan, *supra* note 17.

2 *Id.*

the looting of precious metals from coffins and mummies, and even to robbing the royal corpse. Other texts record carousing on royal burial equipment and blasphemous activity by individuals. Such behavior suggests that at least part of the population had little fear of repercussions from human authorities in this world or from godly ones in the next. Morality was articulated as the sum of actions, good and bad, and as fulfilling social norms, not as faith or piety. Judgment was presented postmortem.[1] The Egyptian dead were judged on the weighted balance between their good and bad actions,[2] depicted as the weighing of the heart after death. The requirement was that their hearts were lighter or equal in weight with the Maat-feather (linked with the goddess Maat, who symbolized justice and truth).

As in the Babylonian age, corruption was found in the Egyptian judiciary.[3] A man's confession dated c.1110 B.C. described not only how the tombs were robbed, but also how easy it was to escape punishment if arrested and return to one's comrades to rob again.[4,5] Pharaonic Egypt was centered around absolute power vested in one person, "Pharaon". Pharaon was the supreme head of state as well as all the authorities, executive, legislative, judicial and religious. Lack of separation of powers resulted in bureaucratic corruption for more than two thousand years of the Pharaonic period.[6] In the late Pharaonic and Ptolemaic periods, in particular, the legislature took over the duties of the judiciary. Pharaon served as supreme judge and the greatest priest. This consequently

1 S.G.F. Brandon, *A Problem of the Osirian Judgment of the Dead*, 5 Numen, fasc. 2, Apr. 1958), at 110, 110-127.

2 The Literature of Ancient Egypt: An Anthology of Stories, Instructions, Stelae, Autobiographies, and Poetry (W.K. Simpson ed., 3d ed. 2003).

3 Hassan El-Saady, Studien zur Altägyptischen Kultur [Considerations on Bribery in Ancient Egypt] 295-304 (1998).

4 Joshua J. Mark, *Tomb Robbing in Ancient Egypt*, Ancient Hist. Encyc. (Jul. 17, 2017), https://www.ancient.eu/article/1095/tomb-robbing-in-ancient-egypt/.

5 J.E. Lewis, The Mammoth Book of Eyewitness Ancient Egypt (2003).

6 Eyre, *supra* note 38.

marked increasing bureaucratic penetration and standardization of process, but did not represent real structural efficiency or consistency.[1]

1.2.3 Ancient China

"A big rooster eats no small rice," and "money falls into the hands of yamen [also known as state office] secretaries". Both these Chinese proverbs show how corruption has left its mark on the Chinese language and culture.[2]

The Criminal Code of the Quin Chinese dynasty (221-207 B.C.) mentions the phenomenon of corruption and records extremely harsh punishments for the practice.[3] Yet power had special implications in the social life of ancient China, because it could enrich an individual in "ways much faster than other avenues". A couple of popular Chinese sayings reveal the special function of power in Chinese society. The first, "sheng guan fa chain", translates to "get promoted and then become rich" and "sannian qinzhifu, shiwan baihuayinw" translates to "a three-year term of office could earn an extra income of 100,000 tales of silver even for a clean magistrate".[4] Surprisingly, the Confucian concept

---

1 *Id.*

2 Peter Burgess, *Corruption*, True Value Metrics (Jan. 16, 2012), http://www.truevaluemetrics.org/DBadmin/DBtxt001.php?vv1=txt00009539.

3 45 Ciprian Rotaru et al., *A Review of Corruption Based on the Social and Economic Evolution of Ancient Greece and Ancient Rome*, 23 Theoretical & Applied Econ., no. 2(607), 2016, at 239.

G.J. Lambsdorff et al., The New Institutional Economics of Corruption. Routledge Publishing (2005).

4 Angel Puente Reyes, Harmony of Confucian Values on Chinese Legal System – A View of the Rule of Law with Chinese Characteristics 2 (2014), *available at* https://www.researchgate.net/publication/279203810_Harmony_of_Confucian_Values_on_Chinese_Legal_System_-_A_view_of_the_Rule_of_Law_with_Chinese_Characteristics.

of *renzhi* or "people's government" largely contributed to widespread corruption throughout China.[1] In Confucian's view, a true and honest state bureaucrat should be guided by moral principles[2] and therefore, striving for material wealth was considered inappropriate. However, this was not seen in practice. Wang Anshi, the famous Chinese economist of the Song dynasty, wanted to introduce reforms in monetary institutions that would reduce corruption and nepotism, but his ideas were dismissed by the Confucian elite.[3] As a result, corruption continued to exist on an even larger scale, involving the court itself and the local elite. In practice, it meant that the more important an issue was, the deeper one would need to reach into one's pocket. During the Ming Dynasty, a powerful bureaucrat did not believe, even when in jail, that he would be sentenced, because of a nepotistic sentiment: "all the senior officials of the royal court are my friends and relatives". It is notable that according to Confucius, a good minister is "one who follows the way, he does not follow the rules".[4]

1.2.4 Ancient Greece[5]

In ancient Greece, corruption was often equated with violating the law to ensure personal advantage. Both Plato and Thucydides offer portraits of the perfect city, but then point towards corruption required in such cities. Without corruption, they argue, these cities cannot maintain perfection, as they suffer transformations in a world

1 Ojesbi Jung Shahi, China Fight Against Corruption (2016).

2 Wang An Shih: Practical Reformer? xii (J. Meskill ed., 1963); *see also* F.W. Mote, Imperial China, 900–1800 141-42 (1999).

3 András Csuka, *Long History of Corruption in China*, GB Times (May 6, 2016), https://gbtimes.com/long-history-corruption-china.

4 Simon Leys ed., The Analects of Confucius. New York: W.W. Norton (1997). p193.

5 Rotaru et al., *supra* note 46, at 239-248.

of constant change. Socrates, according to Athenian accusations, corrupted the youth of Athens, urging them not to support the political agenda of the city any longer. Both the Athenians and Socrates attempted to eliminate the cause of potential corruption, Socrates by the power of the word and the Athenians by putting Socrates to death.[1] According to Demosthenes, a Greek statesman and orator of ancient Athens, those who accepted bribes, or who offered them, or corrupted others through promises at the expense of people in general or any citizen, were punished by the Athenian law by deprivation of rights. Their possessions were confiscated and the same punishment was applied to their sons.[2] Corruption was one of the most serious crimes. In ancient Greece, to reduce the scourge of corruption, Plato proposed capital punishment for officials or dignitaries who accepted gifts to do their duties. The rise of corruption damaged the prestige of priests and the sanctuary. Priests of Delphi oracles held a privileged position and influenced the course of Greek policy.[3]

One of the most notable measures against corruption and the accumulation of wealth was passed in Sparta by the legislator Lycurgus, a legendary lawgiver who took steps to eliminate inequality and differences in the wealth of the Spartans. When aristocrats resisted, he withdrew all gold and silver money from circulation and ordered the exclusive use of iron money. He then gave an insignificant value to even large amounts of iron, so any decent quantity of the new currency required a large space for storage in the home and an ox cart for transport. For those who might have wanted to gather, steal, or receive bribes or plunder, these iron bars would have been

---

1 45. *Id.*
W.A. Saxonhouse, *To Corrupt: The Ambiguity of the Language of Corruption in Ancient Athens, in* Corruption: Expanding the Focus (B. Hindess et al. eds., 2013).

2 L. Hill, *Conceptions of Political Corruption in Ancient Athens and Rome*, 34 Hist. Pol. Thought 565 (2013).

3 M. Costas, Grecia Partenonului (2001).

impossible to hide. Additionally, because they could not be used outside of Sparta, their value was null and void in the rest of Greece. So, when these iron bars became the currency, earnings inequality disappeared from Lacedaemon.[1]

A robust bid to eradicate corruption and bribery in the state was also made by the Archon (Greek ruler). His oath upon taking office included the obligation not to accept bribes. Furthermore, any magistrate who was caught and convicted of bribery was bound to a gold statue in Delphi weighing the equivalent of the silver of the bribe money received. The ratio of gold to silver is 10:1, so these unfortunate individuals paid tenfold, through this old formula, for their bribe-taking.[2]

Another aspect of anti-corruption is shown in the behavior of the Greek ambassador from Thebes, Pelopidas. In order to maintain relations with the Persian king Artaxerxes, the Thebans and Athenians sent their ambassadors to his court. The Thebans' ambassadors were led by Pelopidas. Pelopidas, who had managed a win against the Spartans, was a favorite at the Persian court. Artaxerxes showered him with attention and honored him with gifts. Pelopidas, however, simply accomplished his diplomatic goals and returned to Thebes without accepting any of the gifts.[3] Subsequently, the Athenians convicted and executed their ambassador Timagoras, who had accepted gifts from Artaxerxes. Since these gifts were considered bribes and it was immoral to benefit from the enemy, he had officially abused his position for personal gain.[4]

---

1 Plutarch, Lives. Vol. I: Theseus and Romulus, Lycurgus and Numai, Solon and Publicola (Macmillan 1914).

2 Hill, *supra* note 56, at XX.

3 Plutarch, Lives. Vol. VII: Demosthenes and Cicero, Alexander and Caesar (Harvard Univ. Press 1967).

4 Hill, *supra* note 56, at XX.

1.2.5 Ancient Rome[1]

Under the ancient Roman system of rule, the resources of the vast Roman empire, including its law and religion, were used for senators' interests. The senate controlled the supreme court and judiciary committees, which had been established to judge acts of corruption by the senators themselves. But the senators, who saw their peers' behavior as natural, did not see a problem. Bribing voters was a common practice, but an even more perfidious form of corruption began to spread, in the form of fights with gladiators in arena shows, which represented the price paid for popularity by those who held the power of the State.[2] A law called Cincia de Donis et Muneribus was passed in 204 B.C., forbidding lawyers and magistrates from receiving any kind of payment or gifts for services offered, and regulating restitution. The law was updated and expanded in the imperial era under Augustus, Claudius and Nero.[3] But rampant corruption, despite the law, obliged republican Rome to adopt a series of laws to combat this scourge. These were the Calpurnia (149 B.C.), Acilia (123 B.C.), Servilia (110 B.C.), Cornelia (81 B.C.) and Yulia Repetundarum (59 B.C.).[4] Where laws were disobeyed more frequently than they were observed, the corruption of people of influence destabilized the administrative system and had a negative impact on the growth and welfare of the republic.[5] The first known case of a Roman official taking bribes occurred in 171 B.C., when a senator was exposed for taking handouts from a foreign diplomat in exchange for political favors. Neither had enough money to pay off all of those who came to

1 *Id.*

2 *Id.*

3 A. Lintott, *Electoral Bribery in the Roman Republic*, 80 J. Roman Stud. 1-16 (1990).

4 H.J. Swithinbank, *The Corruption of the Constitution: The Lex Gabinia and Lex Manilia and the Changing Res Publica*, *in* Corruption and Integrity in Ancient Greece and Rome (P. Bosman ed., 2012).

5 W.L. Collins, Cicero (1873).

know about the agreement and the news went public. Unfortunately, after this event, bribery became the norm in the republic's foreign relations. As far as voting was concerned, a law was passed in 181 B.C. which declared that any candidate who was caught campaigning illegally would be ineligible to run for any political position for ten years.

To summarize, corruption existed in all ancient civilizations. There is a collective consensus that corruption is represented by actions deemed to be unacceptable and against common sense. Any act that prevents others from enjoying what is supposed to be granted is corruption.

Corruption also varies according to group/social standards. As time passes, it manifests in real life situations or in stories about people or ideas, as shown in the above-mentioned dynasties, and it is a serious and dangerous problem.

1.3 NON-SECULAR DERIVATIVES

Just as water can get contaminated; spirit does too!

From a religious angle, corruption was envisaged as contamination, a lack of virtue from a moral perspective and a decay of spirit expressed through disobedience towards God. There is extensive literature in every major faith — Judaism, Christianity and Islam — on values and legal codes of conduct; on the managing of business and the workplace; on the accumulation and use of wealth.

Statistics show that more than 50% of people hold a belief or religion,[1] and two of the Abrahamic religions have scored the highest percentages in terms of followers. It is therefore important to discuss

1 *These Are All the World's Major Religions in One Map*, World Econ. Forum (Mar. 26, 2019), https://www.weforum.org/agenda/2019/03/this-is-the-best-and-simplest-world-map-of-religions.

corruption in a religious context, since many people can identify with anti-corruption statements found within the three major monotheistic faiths.

In Judaism, the sources are The Torah, The Talmud and The Midrash. In Christianity, they are The Old Testament and The New Testament.[1] In Islam, the basis of codes and laws of conduct is the holy scripture, The Quran, the teachings of which are exemplified in the sayings and life of the Prophet Mohammed (The Hadith).

Regardless of the corruption manifested in society, the three monotheistic religions renounce corrupt actions and practices and punish those involved in them. In order to grasp the idea of corruption from a non-secular perspective, a non-exhaustive set of illustrations from the business sector will be discussed, focusing on bribery, fraud, cheating, discrimination and other forms of corruption.

From a religious perspective, bribery is a sin. It corrupts conscience and perverts justice. Forms of corruption other than bribery are also considered immoral in religious scriptures.

Religious texts which show how corruption was recognized and rejected will also be discussed. Instances of corruption according to Judaism, Christianity and Islam will be presented in chronological order.

1.3.1 Judaism

The book of Psalms 26:10: "In whose hands is craftiness, and their right hand is full of bribes"; the book of Exodus 23:8: "And thou shalt take no gift; for a gift blinds them that have sight, and perverts the words of the righteous"[2] and the book of Isaiah 1:21-23: "Thy princes are rebellious, and companions of thieves; every one loveth bribes, and followeth after rewards; they judge not the fatherless, neither

---

1 John Drane, The Bible as Library (BBC UK 2011).

2 Munir Quddus et al., *Business Ethics – Perspectives from Judaism, Christianity and Islam*, Proceedings of the Midwest Business Economics Association (2005).

doth the cause of the widow come unto them". These examples showcase how bribery was viewed in Jewish religious texts. It is clear from Leviticus 19:11 that cheating was an unacceptable act: "Ye shall not steal; neither shall ye deal falsely, nor lie one to another". Moreover, cheating (defrauding by deceitful means) was also condemned in Amos 8:4-8: "Hear this, O ye that would swallow the needy, and destroy the poor of the land". Other forms of unjust treatment were warned against in Deuteronomy 24:14: "Thou shalt not oppress a hired servant that is poor and needy, whether he be of thy brethren, or of thy strangers that are in thy land within thy gates". This verse promotes non-discrimination. As mentioned earlier, corruption is considered to be moral decay, which is explicitly referred to in Genesis 6:11: "And the earth was corrupt before God, and the earth was filled with violence".

1.3.2 Christianity

In the Christian New Testament, Simon the sorcerer tried to buy the power that he perceived in the laying on of hands by the apostles, and Simon Peter chastised him, in Acts 8:20: "But Peter said unto him, thy money perish with thee, because thou hast thought that the gift of God may be purchased with money". The essence of the offence was addressed by Peter in the words: "because thou hast thought that the gift of God may be purchased with money".

All people are considered important and are to be treated fairly; the New Testament cautions against making distinctions between people based on wealth, real or imagined. Also, in the Old Testament, it is stated in Proverbs 29:2 (CSB): "When the righteous flourish, the people rejoice, but when the wicked rule, people groan", and in 28:15: "Like a roaring lion or a charging bear is a wicked ruler over a poor people".

1.3.3 Islam

The holy Quran, in verse ("aya") 188 of Surat Al Baqara, says:

> *And do not consume one another's wealth unjustly or send it [in bribery] to the rulers in order that [they might aid] you [to] consume a portion of the wealth of the people in sin, while you know [it is unlawful].*[1]

Moreover, in the sayings of the Prophet Mohammed, there is specific mention of bribes: "the person who gives a bribe and the person who takes a bribe, both will burn in hell". In Islamic writings, a great deal of emphasis is placed on honest dealings. The government or authority is charged with ensuring that traders don't defraud their customers in weights, etc. The Quran is strict in making the point that traders and businesses who indulge in fraud are committing a sin in the eyes of God: "God permits trade but forbids usurious gain" (Quran 2:275).[2] "Give just measure and weight, nor withhold from the people the things that are their due" (Quran 11:85)[3] and "He who cheats is not one of us" (saying of the Prophet Mohammed). Discrimination based on race, ethnicity, etc., is generally considered abhorrent in the teachings of all faiths, and the Islamic scriptures on discrimination are clear. All forms of discrimination are considered unjust and are opposed in private business and the public domain, as explicitly stated in the Quran: "O mankind! We created you from a single (pair) of male and female, and made you into nations and tribes, that you may know each other" (Quran 49:13),[4] and also in the Prophetic saying:

1 *Consumption of What is Unlawful Corrupts the Hearts*, Islamweb, https://www.islamweb.net/amp/en/article/180469/ (last visited October 27, 2021)

2 *Surat Al Baqarah*, Ayah 275, Pages 2–49, Quran.com, https://quran.com/2/275?translations=85,101,19,22,20 (last visited October 27, 2021)

3 *Surat Hud*, Ayah 85, pages 221–235, Quran.com, https://quran.com/11/85?translations=31,20,19,101,85,95,18,84 (last visited October 27, 2021)

4 *Surat Al-Hujurat*, Ayah 13, Pages 515–517, Quran.com, https://quran.com/49:13?font=v1&translations=149,167,84,95,19,22,206,20,203 (last visited October 27, 2021)

No Arab has superiority over any non-Arab and no non-Arab has any superiority over an Arab; no dark person has superiority over a white person and no white person has a superiority over a dark person. The criterion for honor in the sight of God is righteousness and honest living.

There is an explicit mention of corruption in the Quran 2:205 (Surat Al Baqara): "But whenever he prevails, he goes about the earth spreading corruption and destroying [man's] tilth and progeny: and God does not love corruption".[1]

***

Just as it is impossible not to taste the honey (or the poison) that finds itself at the tip of the tongue, so it is impossible for a government servant not to eat up, at least a bit of the king's revenue.

Kautilya wrote these words thousands of years ago. The sentiment continues to be true, and although politicians in various countries have not always historically spurned corruption, yet most modern governments nowadays do. At long last, religion and politics are closer to an agreement on corruption, even as they continue to evolve. All religions, regardless of their provenance, condemn what is evil and praise the good, and the law in every nation does so too. Corruption has been declared to be one of the worst diseases of mankind[2] and it is perceived as a problem that discredits governments.[3]

---

1 Surat Al-Baqaraht , Ayah 205, Pages 2–49, Quran.com, https://quran.com/2:205?font=v1&translations=149,171,17,85,95,206,20,207 (last visited October 27, 2021)

2 Stated in President of the World Bank, James D. Wolfensohn's, speech: for developing countries to achieve growth and poverty reduction, "we need to deal with the cancer of corruption". James D. Wolfensohn, World Bank Group, *People and Development: Address to the Board of Governors, Washington, DC, October 1, 1996*, http://documents.worldbank.org/curated/en/243871468141893629/People-and-development-address-to-the-Board-of-Governors-Washington-DC-October-1-1996.

3 Eyre, *supra* note 38.

1.4 DEFINITION OF CORRUPTION

As indicated in the previous section, the phenomenon of corruption has existed for a long time, and therefore the concept of corruption has been dealt with and theorized in various ways. When it comes to defining it, there are three common approaches, particularly in anti-corruption academic literature.

The first approach is to refer to definitions from dictionaries, competent authorities and global organizations. These are trusted resources which have defined corruption after wide exposure to various corruption cases around the world. Moreover, there are a number of scholars who have invented a definition of it based on formulas.

Most dictionaries list the basic meaning of corruption as originating, via middle English and old French, from the Latin *corruptio*. The word is the past participle of *corrumpere*, meaning "mar, bribe, destroy", from *cor* ("altogether") and *rumpere* ("to break"). The Oxford Dictionary defines corruption as:

> *i) dishonest or fraudulent conduct by those in power, typically involving bribery;*
> *ii) the action or effect of making someone or something morally depraved;*
> *iii) the process by which a word or expression is changed from its original state to one regarded as erroneous or debased;*
> *iv) the process by which a computer database or program becomes debased by alteration or the introduction of errors; and/or,*
> *v) the process of decay; putrefaction.*[1]

1 *Corruption*, Lexico, https://www.lexico.com/definition/corruption (last visited Sep. 164, 2019).

Definitions pertaining to the moral decay that corruption may engender are also likely to provide consensus when discussing its effects, but continue to cause difficulty when determining its meaning.[1]

Similarly, in the Cambridge Dictionary: "illegal, bad, or dishonest behavior, especially by people in positions of power". It further defines corruption in business, which will be tackled in later chapters, as the following: "dishonest or illegal behavior involving a person in a position of power, for example, accepting money for doing something illegal or immoral".[2] Likewise, the Merriam-Webster Dictionary defines corruption as:

> *i) dishonest or illegal behavior especially by powerful people (such as government officials or police officers): depravity;*
> *ii) inducement to wrong by improper or unlawful means (such as bribery), the corruption of government officials;*
> *iii) a departure from the original or from what is pure or correct, the corruption of a text, the corruption of computer files; and/or,*
> *iv) decay, decomposition, the corruption of a carcass.*[3]

As far as global organizations and competent authorities are concerned, the United Nations Global Program Against Corruption defines corruption as: "the abuse of power for private gain".[4] Transparency international (TI) describes it as "the abuse

1 G. Brooks et al., *Defining Corruption*, *in* A. Graycar & T. Prenzler, Preventing Corruption: Crime Prevention and Security Management 12 (2013).

2 *Corruption*, Cambridge Dictionary, https://dictionary.cambridge.org/dictionary/english/corruption (last visited Sep. 16, 2019).

3 *Corruption*, Merriam-Webster Dictionary, https://www.merriam-webster.com/dictionary/corruption (last visited Sep. 16, 2019).

4 U.N. Off. Drugs & Crime [UNODC], The Global Program Against Corruption, UN Anti-Corruption toolkit (2d ed. 2004), *available at* https://www.unodc.org/documents/corruption/Toolkit_ed2.pdf.

of entrusted power for private gain".[1] The World Bank identifies corruption as "the use of public office for private gain".[2] The INTERPOL definition of corruption is "any course of action or failure to act by individuals or organizations, public or private, in violation of law or trust for profit or gain".[3] The Organization for Economic Co-operation and Development (OECD) regards corruption as "active or passive misuse of the powers of public officials (appointed or elected) for private financial or other benefits".[4]

The second approach to defining corruption follows the notion that it is impossible to reach unity in defining it. For example, the United Nations' Global Program Against Corruption asserts that there is no single, comprehensive, universally accepted definition.[5] Most scholars and experts in the field have their legitimate and logical reasons for adopting this position. They even limit the definition of corruption to acts of abuse of power by government.[6]

Professor Robert Klitgaard has defined corruption in an equation: Corruption = Monopoly Power + Discretion – Accountability.[7] In

---

1 *Corruption*, Transparency Int'l, https://www.transparency.org/glossary/term/corruption (last visited Oct. 2, 2019).

2 Jeff Huther & Anwar Shah, Anti-Corruption Policies and Programs: A Framework for Evaluation (World Bank 2000).

3 *Corruption*, Interpol, https://www.interpol.int/en/Crimes/Corruption (last visited Apr. 4, 2020); Steve M. Windham, *Corruption in Law Enforcement*, MJ652 Project Presentation on Corporate Crime (Feb. 3, 2008), https://www.slideshare.net/SteveMWindhamLLMMBAE/mj652-corporate-crime-capstone-project-41979073.

4 *Glossary of Statistical Terms: Corruption*, OECD, https://stats.oecd.org/glossary/detail.asp?ID=4773 (last visited Oct.2, 2019).

5 UNODC, *supra* note 77.

6 Li, Y.L., Wu, S.J. and Hu, Y.M. (2011) A Review of Anti-Corruption Studies in Recent China. Chinese Public Administration, 11, 115-119.

7 K. Anukansai, *Corruption: The Catalyst for the Violation of Human Rights*, NACC J., Jul. 2010, at 6 (quoting R. Klitgaard, Controlling Corruption (1988).

addition, he has defined it as misuse of office for unofficial ends.[1] Klitgaard uses this formulation to identify and analyze situations conducive to bureaucratic corruption. Officials can use the prospect of lucrative contracts to extract corrupt payments, for example, if they can exploit a monopoly – power to award contracts not available elsewhere – and discretion – the ability to choose from among bidders.[2]

The United Nations Development Program (UNDP) has this equation: Corruption = (Monopoly Power + Discretion) – (Accountability + Integrity + Transparency).[3]

Some recent analyses have defined corruption as behavior which is opposite to "ethical universalism"[4] or "impartiality" in the exercise of public power. The conceptualization of corruption as officials turning "public goods" into private goods for their own benefit may be a debatable one. However, the approach is useful for its comprehensiveness.[5] The majority of scholars have pointed out "that there are many ways to define corruption in detail. But no definition can be applied to all research purposes".[6]

Defining corruption is complicated, owing to the fact that there is "no fixed disciplinary allegiance", and analysts have ransacked the cupboards of anthropology, economics, organization theory, philosophy, political science and sociology in their efforts to find ways of making the concept more robust and useful.[7]

---

1 Robert Klitgaard, *International Cooperation against Corruption*, 39 SPAN, no. 5, Sept./Oct. 1998, at 38.

2 M. Johnston, Corruption, Contention and Reform: The Power of Deep Democratization 25 (2014).

3 U.N. Dev. Program [UNDP], Anti-Corruption Practice Note (2004).

4 Alina Mungiu-Pippidi, *Corruption: Diagnosis and Treatment*, 17 J. Democracy, Jul. 2006, at 86, 86-99.

5 Bo Rothstein & Jan Teorell, *Defining and Measuring Quality of Government, in* Good Government: The Relevance of Political Science 6-26 (Sören Holmberg & Bo Rothstein eds., 2012).

6 J. Bussell, Greed, Corruption, and the Modern State Essays in Political Economy 22-32 (2015).

7 Robert Williams, *New Concepts for Old?* 20 Third World Q. 503, 503-513 (1999).

The third approach consists of the belief that corruption can be defined through illustrations and examples of its different forms. This will be explored in the next section.

The United Nations Convention Against Corruption (UNCAC) is the most comprehensive international anti-corruption treaty to date. It does not define corruption as such. It rather defines specific acts of corruption and urges states to criminalize these acts in their jurisdictions. It lists a range of corruption offences, including the active and passive bribery of domestic and foreign public officials, obstruction of justice, illicit enrichment and embezzlement.[1]

1.5 FORMS OF CORRUPTION

What are the common forms of corruption? Corruption mutates and comes in numerous forms, on different levels, across all sectors. At least six billion people worldwide live in countries considered to be corruption-ridden. Sixty-eight percent are considered to have serious corruption problems.[2] According to Heidenheimer,[3] corruption has shades, ranging from white through grey to black, depending upon the opinions of elite segments of society as well as mass opinion in different kinds of communities.[4] It is important to be aware of all its shades and forms. This section will deal with various categorizations adopted by different players in the anti-corruption field,

---

1 OECD, Corruption: A Glossary of International Criminal Standards 11-12 (2007).

2 Transparency Int'l, Corruption Perception Index (2015).

3 Political Sciences Professor Heidenheimer, Arnold Joseph was born on November 23, 1929 in Wuerzburg, Bavaria, Germany. He came to the United States in 1940. AB, Cornell University, 1950. Master of Arts, American University, 1952. Doctor of Philosophy, London School of Economics, 1957. *Arnold Heidenheimer*, PraBook, https://prabook.com/web/arnold_joseph.heidenheimer/1698122 (last visited Oct. 2, 2019).

4 Arnold J. Heidenheimer, *Perspectives on the Perception of Corruption, in* A. J. Heidenheimer et al., Political Corruption: A Handbook (1989).

ranging from "petty" to "grand" forms of corruption. Where petty corruption takes place on a small scale, it is often viewed as a mere annoyance. It frequently occurs at the juncture between public officials and the public they are supposed to serve. This may come in the form of accepting small gifts, which are improper, due to the giver's expectation of favors.[1] As for grand corruption, this is corruption which pervades the highest levels of national government, leading to a broad erosion of confidence in good governance, the rule of law and economic stability.[2] As stated earlier, corruption manifests itself in different ways in different circumstances. However, there are some forms of corruption which reoccur in every system. These are grand corruption, petty corruption, active corruption, passive corruption, political corruption, systematic corruption and other unique classifications created by experts in the field.

The Transparency International classification is based on the relative size and frequency of acts, from petty to grand corruption.

1.5.1 Petty Corruption

Petty corruption, as defined by Transparency international (TI), is the everyday abuse of entrusted power by low- and mid-level public officials in their interactions with ordinary citizens, who often are trying to access basic goods or services in places like hospitals, schools, police departments and other agencies. It distorts the functioning of central government.[3] It is a situation where a public official

1 *Petty Corruption*, Legal Dictionary (Jun. 2016), https://legaldictionary.net/corruption/.

2 *See*, e.g., S. Rose-Ackerman, *Democracy and 'Grand Corruption' UNESCO, 1996 (ISSI 149/1996), reprinted in* Explaining Corruption 321-336 (R. Williams ed., 2000).

3 Global Integrity & UNDP Oslo Governance Centre, A User's Guide to Measuring Integrity (2008); *Corruption Glossary*, U4, http://www.u4.no/document/glossary.cfm (last visited Apr. 4, 2020).

demands or expects money for performing an act which he or she is ordinarily required by law to do, or when a bribe is paid to obtain services which the official is prohibited from providing.[1]

1.5.2 Grand Corruption

Grand corruption involving public officials is referred to as kleptocracy.[2] It occurs when a high level government official commits acts which distort policies or the central functioning of the state, enabling him/her to benefit at the expense of the public good.[3] It is a form of corruption which pervades the highest levels of national government, leading to a broad erosion of confidence in good governance, the rule of law and economic stability.[4] Transparency International (TI) defines it as the abuse of high-level power that benefits the few at the expense of the many and causes serious and widespread harm to individuals and society. It often goes unpunished.[5]

1.5.3 Systematic Corruption

This occurs where corruption permeates the whole of society, to the point of being accepted as a means of conducting everyday transactions.[6] It is a situation in which the major institutions and processes

---

1 C. Sandgren, *Combating Corruption: The Misunderstood Role of Law*, 13 Int'l Law. 717 (2005).

2 World Bank, *Unit 1: Introduction to Corruption*, http://siteresources.worldbank.org/PSGLP/Resources/corruptionunit1.pdf (last visited Nov. 4, 2019).

3 Transparency Int'l, The Anti-Corruption Plain Language Guide 23 (2015).

4 *See* C. Maria & K. Haarhuis, Promoting Anti-Corruption Reforms: Evaluating the Implementation of a World Bank Anti-Corruption Program in Seven African Countries (1999-2001) (2005).

5 Transparency Int'l, *supra* note 102.

6 C. Heymans & B. Lipietz, *Corruption and Development: Some Perspectives*, 40 Inst. Sec. Stud. Monograph Series, 1999, at 8.

of the state are routinely dominated and used by corrupt individuals and groups, and in which many people have few practical alternatives to dealing with corrupt officials.[1] It affects institutions and influences individual behavior at all levels of a political and socio-economic system. This type of corruption is embodied in specific socio-cultural environments and tends to be monopolistic, organized and difficult to avoid.[2]

1.5.4 Active/Passive Corruption

The terms active or "meat eaters" and passive or "grass eaters" were coined in relation to corruption by the Commission to Investigate Alleged Police Corruption (known informally as the Knapp Commission, after its chairman Whitman Knapp) in 1970.[3] However, in criminal law terminology, the terms active and passive can be used to distinguish between a particular corrupt action and an attempted or incomplete offence. For example, "active" corruption would include all cases where payment and/or acceptance of a bribe had taken place. It would not include cases where a bribe was offered but not accepted, or solicited but not paid. In the formulation of comprehensive national anti-corruption strategies which combine criminal justice with other elements, such distinctions are less critical. Nevertheless, care should be taken to avoid confusion between the two concepts. In discussions of transactional offences such as bribery, "active bribery" usually refers to the offering or paying of a bribe. According to the meat eaters concept, police officers who aggressively use their position of power to gain personal profits or acquire favors can be referred to as "meat eaters". This would be the form of corruption typically characterized in popular

---

1 *Id.*

2 *Id.* Neil S. Ruskin, *Corrupt Cops: Meat Eaters versus Grass Eaters*, Neil Ruskin Law Firm (Apr. 2016), https://www.neilruskinlawfirm.com/blog/2016/04/corrupt-cops-meat-eaters-versus-grass-eaters/.

3 *Id.*

movies and television shows. A cop shaking down a business owner for protection money or a group of detectives who skim some evidence off the top for their own personal use – these examples typify a meat eater.[1] On the other hand, "passive bribery" refers to the receiving of a bribe.[2] Police officers who do not seek out personal benefits – but also do not wave them off with a "no thanks" – can be considered grass eaters. What's the harm in accepting a free coffee and Danish pastry from the corner market? If nothing else, this officer would not be maintaining the appearance of propriety. Would this shop owner receive preferential treatment in the future? Would the police officer stop by this shop more often than usual, to the detriment of the rest of his "beat"? It's impossible to tell for sure, but the mere fact that these concerns can be raised calls the officer's objectiveness into question.[3]

1.5.5 State Capture Corruption

After the collapse of Communism, almost all transition economies faced the task of building entirely new governance structures and mechanisms. With their policy capacity unbalanced and accountability structures underdeveloped, one would expect them to score high on both counts of corruption — decentralized administrative corruption and centralized state capture. Weak state structures seem to favor both kinds of corruption, whereas strong centralized states create more fertile ground for state capture than for administrative corruption.

State capture suggests that the system acts massively and deliberately to set the rules of the game in ways that maximize rent-seeking behavior for those enjoying political power. Under these circumstances, corruption feeds on itself by fueling counterproductive,

1 *Id.*

2 *See, e.g.*, Criminal Law Convention on Corruption, arts. 2-3. E.T.S. no 173 (Jan. 27, 1999).

3 Ruskin, *supra* note 108.

corruption-generating regulations.[1] The World Bank has intensively debated corruption and two of the most reoccurring themes were administrative corruption and state capture.

i) Administrative or bureaucratic corruption

While state capture encodes advantages for particular individuals or groups in the basic legal or regulatory framework, administrative corruption refers to the intentional imposition of distortions in the prescribed implementation of existing laws, rules and regulations, to provide advantages to either state or non-state actors, as a result of the illicit and non-transparent provision of private gains to public officials. The classic example of administrative corruption is that of a hapless shop owner forced to pay bribes to a seemingly endless stream of official inspectors, so that they will overlook minor (or possibly major) infractions of existing regulations. Beyond such forms of extortion, administrative corruption also includes familiar examples, such as "grease payments" — bribes to gain licenses, smooth customs procedures, win public procurement contracts, or to be given priority in the provision of a variety of other government services. Finally, state officials can simply misdirect public funds under their control for their own or their families' direct financial benefit. At the root of this form of corruption is discretion on the part of public officials to grant selective exemptions, to prioritize the delivery of public services, or to discriminate in the application of rules and regulations.[2] Bureaucratic corruption denotes the circumvention of laid down rules and establishes procedures within the performance of responsibilities of public office to obtain

1 Antoni Z. Kamiński[B/] & Bartlomiej Kamiński, *Governance and Corruption in Transition: The Challenge of Subverting Corruption* 6-7 (U.N. Econ. Comm'n Eur., Seminar Paper, 2001).

2 World Bank, Anti Corruption in Transition: A Contribution to the Policy Debate xvii (2000), *available at* https://siteresources.worldbank.org/INTWBIGOVANTCOR/Resources/contribution.pdf.

personal gain, usually monetary.[1]

ii) State capture or selling the state

State capture is defined firstly as the efforts of firms to shape the very institutional environment in which they operate, and secondly, as public procurement corruption, the payment of kickbacks for securing public contracts.[2] In an extreme case, a single powerful monopoly could generate a much higher level of state capture than a larger number of less powerful firms competing to buy off state officials.

1.5.6 Arnold Heidenheimer Typology

Heidenheimer isolated three ideal-types of corruption: public office-centered, market-centered and public interest-centered.

i) Public office-centered

behavior which deviates from the formal duties of a public role because of private-regarding (close family, personal, private clique) pecuniary or status gains; or violates rules against the exercise of certain types of private-regarding influence.[3]

ii) Market-centered

a corrupt civil servant [or business administrator – added by Gallup] regards his (public) office as a [separate] business, the income of which he will seek to maximize. The office then becomes a maximizing unit. The size of his income depends upon the market situation and his talents for finding the point of maximal gain on the public's [or clients'] demand curve.[4]

---

1 U. Mohammed, *Corruption in Nigeria: A Challenge to Sustainable Development in the Fourth Republic*, 9 Eur. Sci. J., no. 4, 2013, at 118.

2 Daniel Kaufmann, Seize the State, Seize the Day: An Empirical Analysis of State Capture and Corruption in Transition Economies Abstract (2000).

3 Joseph S. Nye, *Corruption and Political Development: A Cost-Benefit Analysis*, 61 Am. Pol. Sci. Rev., no. 2, June 1967.

4 Jacob van Klaveren, *The Concept of Corruption*, *in* A. J. Heidenheimer et al., Politi-

iii) Public interest-centered

a pattern of corruption can be said to exist whenever a power-holder who is charged with doing certain things, i.e. who is a responsible functionary or officeholder, is induced to perform corrupt acts by monetary or other rewards not legally provided for.[1]

1.5.7 Johnston Classification[2]

Michael Johnston described four corruption syndromes called "influence markets", "elite cartels", "oligarchs and clans" and "official moguls". These syndromes and the names suggesting their distinctive aspects reflect frequently encountered combinations of stronger or weaker participation of institutions.

i) Influence markets

Indicates access to, and influence within, strong state institutions; often politicians serve as middlemen, putting their connections out for rent in exchange for contributions both legal and otherwise.[3]

ii) Elite cartels (a.k.a Big Men)

Where democratic institutions are weaker, politics and markets become more competitive, and networks of elites use corrupt incentives and exchanges to shore up their positions.[4]

iii) Oligarchs and clans

In cases of major political and economic liberalization with

---

cal Corruption: A Handbook 28 (1989).

1 C. J. Friedrich, *Political Pathology*, 37 Pol. Q., Jan. 1966, at 70.

2 Johnston based his four syndromes on the following questions: what are the links between political and economic liberalization, the strength or weakness of state, political and social institutions, and the kinds of corruption societies experience? What syndromes of corruption result from various combinations of these influences and how do they differ? What kinds of reform are – and are not – appropriate for contrasting corruption problems? *See* Johnston, *supra* note 86, at 2, 36.

3 *Id.* at 42, 60 ("Influence Markets: Influence for Rent, Decisions for Sale").

4 *Id.* at 43, 89.

poorly integrated transitions, weak public-private boundaries have opened up a wide variety of opportunities for corruption, in a context of weak institutions.[1]

iv) Official moguls
Institutions are very weak, the political system remains undemocratic or is opening up only slowly, but the economy is being liberalized at least to a degree. Civil society is weak or non-existent. Opportunities for enrichment and new risks for the already wealthy abound, but political power is personal and often used with impunity. Here, the entrepreneurs with most leverage, or their clients, will be top political figures. Officials may become economic moguls; would-be moguls need official backing.[2]

Other scholars, like Mark Robinson, identify three forms of corruption: firstly, "incidental" corruption, which is confined to wrongdoing on the part of the individual. This takes place in the covert form of bribery by abusing one's position, with the intention of gaining an undue advantage from the public servant. Secondly, "institutional" corruption refers to certain institutions that may be riddled with corruption, due largely to the absence of controls; and lastly, "systemic" corruption reflects situations where corruption is deeply entrenched and pervasive throughout society.[3] Robinson also refers to political corruption, which is the manipulation of policies, institutions and rules of procedure in the allocation of resources and financing by political decision makers, who abuse their position to sustain their power, status and wealth.[4] Further, another dichotomy is "centralized" and "decentralized" corruption, depending on the level of control exercised by the political

1 *Id.* at 44, 120.

2 *Id.* at 46, 155.

3 M. Robinson, Corruption and Development 1–14 (1998).

4 *Anti-Corruption Glossary*, Transparency Int'l, https://www.transparency.org/glossary/ (last visited Nov. 4, 2019).

elite over local officials.[1] Different behaviors have been identified as constituting corruption. These include "bribery,[2] extortion,[3] abuse of office,[4] fraud,[5] embezzlement,[6] money laundering[7] and nepotism".[8,9]

---

1 P. Bardhan, *The Economist's Approach to the Problem of Corruption*, 34 World Dev. 341, 341–48. (2006).

2 Bribery refers to the offering, giving, soliciting, or receiving of any item of value as a means of influencing the actions of an individual holding a public or legal duty. *See Bribery*, Legal Info. Inst., https://www.law.cornell.edu/wex/bribery (last visited Nov. 2, 2019).

3 Forcing action or obtaining something by illegal means. Anyone may commit extortion through force or coercion. A public or private official may also commit extortion under the color of office. *Extortion*, Legal Info. Inst., https://www.law.cornell.edu/wex/extortion (last visited Nov. 2, 2019).

4 A person acting or purporting to act in an official capacity or taking advantage of such actual or purported capacity commits a misdemeanor, knowing that his or her conduct is illegal. *See* 25 C.F.R. § 11.448.

5 *Fraud* is deliberately deceiving someone else with the intent of causing damage. This damage need not be physical damage, in fact, it is often financial. There are many different types of fraud, for example bankruptcy fraud, credit card fraud, and healthcare fraud. The precise legal definition of fraud varies by jurisdiction and by the specific fraud offense. *Fraud*, Legal Info. Inst., https://www.law.cornell.edu/wex/fraud (last visited Nov. 2, 2019).

6 Fraudulent taking of personal property by someone to whom it was entrusted. Most often associated with the misappropriation of money. Embezzlement can occur regardless of whether the defendant keeps the personal property or transfers it to a third party. *Embezzlement*, Legal Info. Inst., https://www.law.cornell.edu/wex/embezzlement (last visited Nov. 2, 2019).

7 Money laundering refers to a financial transaction scheme that aims to conceal the identity, source and destination of illicitly-obtained money; *Money Laundering*, Legal Info. Inst., https://www.law.cornell.edu/wex/money_laundering (last visited Nov. 2, 2019).

8 The act of using your power or influence to get good jobs or unfair advantages for members of your own family; See *Nepotism*, Cambridge Dictionary, https://dictionary.cambridge.org/dictionary/english/nepotism (last visit Nov. 2, 2019).

9 O.J. Otusanya, *Corruption as an Obstacle to Development in Developing Countries: A Review of Literature*, 14 J. Money Laundering Control 387, 387-422 (2011).

This section has offered diverse corruption classifications derived from global recognized institutions in the field, experts in the discipline and competent scholars. In conclusion, it is important to be aware that corruption can be disguised in any of these forms or in completely new garb. The next section will introduce measures that have been put in place to tackle corruption and organizations whose essential mission is to fight it.

CHAPTER TWO: *HOW TO PREVENT CORRUPTION*

2.1 HOW TO DEAL WITH CORRUPTION

The problem of corruption is multi-faceted and the means of combating it are also diverse. There are two main strategies: ex ante (before corruption happens) and ex post (after corruption happens). The former refers to proactive measures in place to prevent corruption from happening. The latter is reactive behavior, the response to corruption after it has happened. These strategies are in alignment with the United Nations Anti-Corruption Convention (UNCAC), which covers the broadest range of corruption offences.[1] Chapter Two (Preventive Measures) reflects the preventive approach and Chapter Three (Criminalization and Law Enforcement) denotes the reactive method. After examining where and when it is best to use anti-corruption tactics, the next section will explore the existing regulatory environment and list all competent global bodies and legislative measures regulating against corrupt practices.

2.1.1 Ex Ante Tactics

The United Nations Convention Against Corruption (UNCAC), in Articles 5 to 14, sets out preventive measures in the following blueprint: policies and practices, preventive anti-corruption bodies,

1 OECD, *supra* note 92, at 11.

public sector and reporting, public procurement and finance management, judiciary and public prosecution, private sector, society participation and money laundering preventive measures. Every state party to the Convention must comply with its standards.

Therefore, before corruption occurs, there is a set of standards and tools in place which will help to eradicate it. These are sunshine laws affecting the fields of finance, information and recruitment, preventive measures of anti-corruption agencies (ACAs), judiciary ethical standards, and a whistleblowing system.

Sunshine laws

An excellent illustration of ex ante tactics is found in what are called "sunshine laws", which require government agencies and bodies to allow the public to attend their meetings and have access to their records.[1] They promote accountability and transparency in government decision making, and in particular, provide a means of obtaining citizen input regarding the development of laws, rules and regulations.[2] Such laws eliminate opportunities for shadowy behavior of any sort, in any sector, using any means. For instance, disclosure of finance and information elements are both important pillars of sunshine laws. Public financial disclosure rules require government officials with decision making powers to periodically disclose the nature and extent of their assets, with the aim of preventing conflict of interest and illicit enrichments and restoring people's trust in the government and national leaders. The same applies in the private sector, yet it is the government which ensures that accounting and auditing standards in the private sector are upheld, and it enforces effective, proportionate and dissuasive civil, administrative and

1 *Sunshine Laws*, U.S. Legal, https://definitions.uslegal.com/s/sunshine-laws/ (last visited Oct. 10, 2019).

2 Sergio Díaz-Briquets & Jorge Pérez-López, Corruption in Cuba: Castro and Beyond 212 (2010).

criminal penalties for failure to comply with such measures.[1] Another important aspect of sunshine laws is the right to access information, which enables citizens to know how the decisions affecting them are made, how public funds are handled, and according to which criteria institutions act. This enables civil society organizations to acquire the information required to develop effective programs and strategies, and to perform their role as watchdogs effectively.[2]

Public services are particularly vulnerable to corruption. They often lack appropriate pre-employment screening and vetting, and post-employment revalidation. This has led to many issues relating to the background of candidates not being checked and has facilitated the practice of 'recycling' employees with problematic discipline, complaint or criminal histories. In many cases, such 'recycled' employees become involved in corruption and/or misconduct in the new agency.[3] Therefore, accessible and objective criteria such as merit and aptitude should serve as the basis of selection, sunshine laws should be in place, principles of efficiency and transparency should be adhered to, in order to promote staff appropriately; and in accordance with the fundamental principles of the legal system, organizations should endeavor to adopt, maintain and strengthen systems for the recruitment, hiring, retention, promotion and retirement of civil servants.[4] As far as the public servant is concerned, it is worth mentioning that the trend of drafting and issuing codes of conduct interchangeably used with a code of ethics is on a rising tide. The foundation of all successful bureaucracies is integrity, objectivity and effectiveness, and most public service codes

---

1 U.N. Convention Against Corruption [UNCAC], art. 12.

2 OECD, Right to Access Information 3 (2018), https://www.oecd.org/mena/governance/right-to-access-information-2018.pdf.

3 *Preventing Corruption*, IBAC Australia, https://www.ibac.vic.gov.au/preventing-corruption (last visited Oct. 10, 2019).

4 UNCAC art. 7.

emphasize these standards.[1] Codes of conduct or codes of behavior are designed to anticipate and prevent certain specific types of behavior, e.g. conflict of interest, self-dealing, bribery and inappropriate actions.[2] These codes come in many forms and are generally designed to address only minimal standards of ethical behavior, emphasizing what one should not do. This helps to deter people from engaging in corrupt practices.

Another important set of laws containing the attributes of sunshine laws are: a) conflict of interest (CoI) regulation and management (and sometimes enforcement), b) rules on gifts received by public officials, c) asset and income disclosure regimes. In carrying out these functions, ACAs may be tasked to conduct administrative investigations (administrative fact-finding) and to propose disciplinary actions against civil servants or high-level officials for breaches of these regimes. A clash between private interests and public professional duties may appear.[3] These conflicts may or may not be connected to monetary gain. Particularly in the human resource management area, they could be related to a multitude of non-pecuniary interests. Having such laws will contribute to preventing corruption in the public sector in general.

Anti-Corruption Agencies (ACAs)

Another element that plays a huge role in the preventive domain of corruption is the ombudsman, as in article 6 (Preventive Anti-Corruption Body or Bodies) of the UNCAC. According to this article, such bodies should be "independent, free from undue

1 Stuart C. Gilman, Ethics Codes and Codes of Conduct as Tools for Promoting an Ethical and Professional Public Service: Comparative Successes and Lessons 13 (2005).

2 *Id.* at 16.

3 UNDP, Methodology for Assessing the Capacities of Anti-Corruption Agencies to Perform Preventive Functions 36 (2011).

influence", just as the ombudsman should be. But what exactly is an ombudsman? He is an individual, a government official (as in Sweden or New Zealand), appointed to receive and investigate complaints made by individuals against abuses or capricious acts of public officials.[1] His role is to protect people against violations of rights, abuse of powers, error, negligence, unfair decisions and maladministration, in order to improve public administration and make the government more accountable for its actions.[2] Going back to article 6, three main characteristics of anti-corruption agencies (ACAs) can be drawn from the text of the Convention. First, the general objective of ACAs is to lower corruption by means of prevention and law enforcement. Second, the operational means of reaching this objective are specified, namely by granting independence and adequate human and financial resources to the agencies to ensure effective functioning, free from undue influence. Finally, according to the UNCAC, the institutional setup can differ in its degree of centralization.[3]

Consequently, in order to facilitate the process of dealing with corruption, it is vital to have as a focal point an organization which tracks anti-corruption matters. Although some countries have launched independent ACAs, others have integrated the obligations into state institutions, including their prosecution agencies,[4] and this is how the UNCAC draws the line between ACAs, as it mentions twice. In article 6, it says about the preventive anti-corruption body or bodies: "Each State Party shall, in accordance with the

1 *Ombudsman*, Merriam-Webster Dictionary, https://www.merriam-webster.com/dictionary/ombudsman (last visited Nov. 2, 2019).

2 Susan Rose-Ackerman, From Elections to Democracy: Building Accountable Government in Hungary and Poland 74 (2005).

3 Annika Engelbert, The Role of Anti-Corruption Agencies in the Investigation and Prosecution of Procurement Related Corruption Cases 2 (2014); *see also* UNCAC arts. 6, 36.

4 *About NACP*, NACP, https://www.iap-association.org/NACP/About-NACP (last visited Nov. 2, 2019).

fundamental principles of its legal system, ensure the existence of a body or bodies, as appropriate, that prevent corruption", and in article 36: "Specialized Authorities: Each State Party shall, in accordance with the fundamental principles of its legal system, ensure the existence of a body or bodies or persons specialized in combating corruption through law enforcement".[1] To be clear, anti-corruption bodies specifically take the middle ground when ex ante/ex poste classifications are involved, because they can perform both duties. Such bodies are sometimes described as "watchdog" or "guard dog" agencies, based on the strength of their investigative powers (i.e. "teeth").[2]

Considering the multitude of anti-corruption institutions worldwide, their various functions and the arguments about their performance, it is difficult to identify all the main patterns and models. Therefore, before examining the duties of ACAs, it will be useful to explore the various types of anti-corruption bodies existing and operating in different countries. Some general observations can be made, based on the different purposes of these institutions. They are: 1. preventive institutions (explained below), 2. law enforcement institutions, 3. multi-purpose anti-corruption agencies (this will be addressed in the ex post section).[3] According to Patrick Meagher, who collected information on some thirty ACAs, the six functions that they commonly perform are: 1. receiving and responding to complaints, 2. intelligence, monitoring and investigation, 3. prosecutions and administrative orders, 4. preventive research, analysis and technical assistance, 5. ethics policy guidance, compliance reviews and scrutiny of asset declarations, 6. public information, education and outreach.[4]

---

1 UNCAC art. 36.

2 B. Anderson, *Guard Dog vs. Watchdog*, Brad Anderson Blog (Jul. 15, 2011), http://www.bradanderson.org/blog/2011/07/guard-dog-vs-watchdog/.

3 *Id.*; *Anti-Corruption Models*, IAP Assoc., https://www.iap-association.org/NACP/Anti-Corruption-Models (last visited Nov. 2, 2019).

4 Patrick Meagher, Anti-Corruption Agencies: A Review of Experience 6 (2002).

As far as ex ante is concerned, institutions may have one or several corruption prevention functions, such as research and analysis, policy development and co-ordination, training and advising various bodies on risks of corruption and available solutions, and other functions. These bodies normally do not have law enforcement powers. However, they may have other specific powers. For instance, agencies reviewing asset declarations of civil servants may have specific powers allowing them to access confidential information.[1]

Preventive institutions are the broadest model. They can be broken down into three main categories: a) anti-corruption coordinating councils, b) dedicated corruption prevention bodies, c) public institutions.[2] Anti-corruption councils are not usually permanent institutions, but operate through regular meetings, and they are often supported by permanent secretariats. Such bodies are usually created to lead the anti-corruption reform efforts in the country. In particular, they help in the development, implementation and monitoring of a national anti-corruption strategy. Anti-corruption councils consist of accountable government agencies and ministries, representatives of executive, legislative and judicial branches of power, and they may involve civil society. An example is the inter-ministerial working group in Albania and its secretariat within the Cabinet of Ministers. Yet it is important to highlight the fact that anti-corruption strategies are mostly drafted by the competent governmental authority. In the state of Qatar, for example, the Administrative Control and Transparency Authority is an independent and permanent authority that has a mandate to develop and implement the national strategy to promote transparency and integrity.[3] It is an

---

1 OECD, Specialized Anti-Corruption Institutions: Review of Models 12 (2008), https://www.oecd.org/corruption/acn/39971975.pdf.

2 *Id.*; *Anti-Corruption Models*, *supra* note 151.

3 *Mandates and Competencies*, Admin. Control & Transparency Auth., https://www.acta.gov.qa/en/mandates-and-competences-of-acta/ (last visited Nov. 2, 2019).

independent and permanent anti-corruption body, representing the second type of preventive ACAs. In general, it is important to be aware of the fact that exceptions and other ACA manifestations and variations exist around the world, and duties can sometimes intertwine.

As mentioned above, dedicated corruption prevention bodies are permanent and have a broad mandate. They are explicitly created for the prevention of corruption and are entrusted with the coordination of anti-corruption strategies, but possess other functions too, such as anti-corruption awareness raising, education, conflict of interest prevention and anti-corruption assessment of legal acts. An example is the Central Service for the Prevention of Corruption (France).[1]

As far as anti-corruption education and awareness is concerned, it is important also to highlight the fact that there are bodies which have fully-fledged anti-corruption education and awareness plans, such as ROLACC, the Rule of Law and Anti-Corruption Center in Qatar. ROLACC is a center based on the ideals of mutual cooperation and partnership building, with an international mandate to spread awareness and knowledge of the policies and tools necessary to prevent and combat corruption. It aims to promote the latest methods and best practices currently available, in order to address corruption and abuses of the rule of law, through capacity building and training.[2]

The third form of preventive ACAs is public institutions. Some countries have created dedicated bodies to deal with issues related to the prevention of corruption, including prevention of conflicts of interest, ethics, integrity and control of asset declarations in the public administration or parliament. An example is the Parliamentary

1 *Id.*; *Anti-Corruption Models*, *supra* note 151.

2 *About Us*, Rule of Law & Anti-Corruption Center, https://www.rolacc.qa/about-us/ (last visited Nov. 2, 2019).

Commissioner for Standards in the House of Commons in the United Kingdom.[1] Similarly, Supreme Audit Institutions (SAI) strengthen good governance, improve human resources management and contribute to national efforts to combat corruption.[2] Acting on citizens' concerns in Oman, the State Financial and Administrative Audit Institution (SFAAI) launched a smart phone-based complaints window to facilitate communication with the community. This has contributed to the detection of many administrative and financial irregularities, and there has been an increase in the number of cases brought to trial for fraudulent activities and in the recovery of public funds. Most importantly, through the use of technology, the SAI has bolstered the public's faith in the government's commitment to eradicate corruption and malpractices and improve transparency.[3] Public finance management (PFM) is another aspect that is often led by ministries of finance. The advantages of addressing PFM and corruption together is that the matter to be investigated is fairly easily identifiable – it is financial resources, whether and how they are raised and how they are spent.[4]

One final important aspect of ACAs is their impact. In other words, how effective and transparent are they? Are they 'see-through entities'? In a more structured manner, the following questions set by the TI frame the issue of the competency of ACAs:

- Is the agency head free of political control in day-to-day operations?

1 *Anti-Corruption Models, supra* note 151.

2 Int'l Org. of Supreme Audit Inst. Capacity Building Soc'y, Strengthening Supreme Audit Institutions: A Guide for Improving Performance 10 (2019), https://www.intosaicbc.org/wp-content/uploads/2019/08/Strengthening_SAIs_ENG-5.pdf.

3 *Id.* at 28.

4 Arne Disch et al., Anti-Corruption Approaches: Literature Review 28 (2009), https://www.sida.se/contentassets/3f5c8afd51a6414d9f6c8f8425fb935b/anti-corruption-approaches-a-literature-review_3153.pdf.

- Are other staff free from political interference and "no go" areas?
- Are staff adequately trained and remunerated?
- Is the office of the head of state effectively within the ACA's jurisdiction?
- Is the agency accountable to all branches of government and the public?
- Are staff subject to integrity reviews and tests, and can doubtful members be removed quickly?[1]

Answering the above questions can help in detecting irregularities if they exist. For instance, take question no. 6. Are staff subject to integrity reviews and tests, and can doubtful members be removed quickly? If the answer is yes, then this is a sign of a healthy agency. If the answer is no, there may be a defect in governance, which requires an immediate intervention to maintain a healthy and non-corrupt environment.

Another detailed analysis was summarized in a UNDP Guide,[2] which addresses capacity development through three distinct but interconnected levels: the enabling environment, the organizational level and the individual level.[3] Enabling environment means that the agency enjoys the required authority to practice what it preaches, in terms of coordinating, overseeing and monitoring other institutions. It exists in harmony with other institutions in the ecosystem and matters are orchestrated with no hurdles, authority overlaps or duplications. Finally, the ACA should be independent. Independence is crucial to fulfilling the enabling

---

1 Meagher, *supra* note 152, at 13.

2 UNDP, Practitioner's Guide: Capacity Assessment of Anti-Corruption Agencies 27-41 (2011), https://www.undp.org/content/dam/undp/library/Democratic%20Governance/IP/Practicioners_guide-Capacity%20Assessment%20of%20ACAs.pdf.

3 *Id.* at 15.

environment element. This is explicitly stated in article 6 of the UNCAC:

> *each State Party shall grant the body or bodies [that prevent corruption] the necessary independence, in accordance with the fundamental principles of its legal system, to enable the body or bodies to carry out its or their functions effectively and free from any undue influence.*

ACAs should not have any undue influence and they are therefore required to report to the highest entity in the country, either the president or parliament. Examining an ACA's organizational level more closely, *how* do things happen inside it? What is the mission and vision of the agency? Is it clear and publicly available? If so, then do its internal policies and mandates serve the institution's vision and mission? The organizational structure and human resources management of ACAs cascade down to very specific details, such as appointments, retention, development, evaluation and dismissal. All of these should meet clear, public standards. Otherwise, the organization will need another anti-corruption institution to deal with it, and the loop will continue to evolve endlessly. The core element of assessment of ACAs boils down to the level of the individual employee, a fundamental component which might tear down an entire ACA system if skills, experience and knowledge are not found there, or if nepotism, *wasta*[1] and other negative factors are involved in their appointment.

---

1 "In Arabic, *wasta* is a common practice and a social norm. People use their family or social contacts to skip the line and gain quicker and better access to schools, universities, hospitals or jobs, and to 'speed up' government paperwork such as ID renewals or birth certificates. How much you can increase the speed and quality of your service often depends on who you know – the higher the better, of course". *WASTA: How Personal Connections Are Denying Citizens Opportunities and Basic Services*, Transparency Int'l (Dec. 11, 2019), https://www.transparency.org/news/feature/wasta_how_personal_connections_are_denying_citizens_opportunities_services.

Judiciary Ethical Standards

People resort to the judiciary to gain justice, so if the judiciary is corrupt, then they are doomed. It is therefore essential that those dispensing justice should adhere to the highest ethical standards. There are various preventive (ex ante) measures in place relating to the judiciary and prosecution services. The UNCAC stipulates the necessity of having internal integrity/ethics units in ministries and public bodies to promote or enforce anti-corruption and ethical rules from within these bodies. Such measures sometimes include rules with respect to the conduct of members of the judiciary.[1] Whilst independence and transparency are viewed as the most crucial prerequisites for judicial integrity, other factors come into play. These include, notably, the funding of jurisdictions, the quality of case and court management, the capacity and training of judicial personnel and their remuneration, and last but not least the existence and enforcement of professional standards[2] and development of codes of conduct for judges and other types of judicial personnel. This is, for instance, the case in Canada, Estonia, Serbia, the UK and the US. In case of non-respect, disciplinary sanctions apply. An example is the Model Code of Judicial Conduct adopted by the American Bar Association.[3] In summary, the judiciary plays a huge role in the broader accountability function. An effective judiciary guarantees fairness in legal processes[4] as it is entrusted with upholding rights and punishing representatives of other branches when they act in contravention of the law. Yet beneath these apparent complexities lie commonalities

1 UNCAC art. 11.

2 *About Consultative Council of European Judges (CCJE)*, Council of Europe, www.coe.int/t/dghl/cooperation/ccje/textes/avis_en.asp (last visited Dec. 12, 2019).

3 Basel Inst. on Governance, Review Report on Strategic Approaches to Corruption Prevention in the OSCE Region by Gretta Fenner Zinkernagel, Managing Director (2012), https://www.osce.org/eea/93468?download=true.

4 *Judiciary*, Transparency Int'l, https://www.transparency.org/topic/detail/judiciary (last visited Dec. 12, 2019).

that point to reforming[1] and protecting the system from the consequences of corruption before it actually happens, through various means such as appointing judges on merit, clear codes of conduct, and fair and effective dismissal procedures for corrupt judges.

In a similar manner, there are also codes that address the public sector; for example, the International Code of Conduct for Public Officials, adopted in resolution 51/59 at the fifty-first session of the UN general assembly in 1997.[2] This code covers a large number of corrupt practices, such as conflict of interest and disqualifications (in article 2), the obligation of asset disclosure (article 3), acceptance of gifts and other favors (article 4); and it extends to political activities as well (article 6), stating that all activities of public officials should be conducted in accordance with the law and administrative policies, and not impair public confidence in the impartial performance of their functions and duties.[3]

Whistleblowing

The impact of the whistleblowing system can make it a dangerous tool, provoking retaliation. This is because, in simple terms, whistleblowing means telling on bad people's actions and naturally bad people will retaliate as soon as they get the chance. A whistleblower is someone that blows the whistle, i.e. they call out, or report, someone else's wrongdoing. He/she is a person working within an organization who reports that organization's misconduct. The person can be a current or past employee. Also, note that the misconduct can be a past act, can be ongoing, or in the planning stages.[4] This system is regulated either by a standalone law, such as the

1 Transparency Int'l, Global Corruption Report (2013).

2 G.A. Res. A/RES/51/59, International Code of Conduct for Public Officials (Jan. 28, 1997).

3 *Id.* art. 6.

4 *What Is the Whistleblower Act? – Definition, Rights & Protection*, Study.com, https://study.com/academy/lesson/what-is-the-whistleblower-act-definition-rights-protection.html (last visited Nov. 2, 2019).

Whistleblower Protection Enhancement Act of 2012, or it can be regulated within a larger context and embedded inside another law, such as the UNCAC. The importance of whistleblowing in the prevention and fight against corruption is widely recognized. As a consequence, provisions on public reporting and the legal protection of reporting persons have been incorporated in several international instruments, including in article 33 of the UNCAC, which says of the protection of reporting persons:

> *Each State Party shall consider incorporating into its domestic legal system appropriate measures to provide protection against any unjustified treatment for any person who reports in good faith and on reasonable grounds to the competent authorities any facts concerning offences established in accordance with this Convention.*

This system operates as a preventive measure, since it can prevent further corruption implications. For instance, Cisco settled with federal, state and local agencies for $8.6 million, in a first-of-its-kind whistleblower case involving cybersecurity issues.[1] A flaw was detected by an employee of Cisco Systems, a software engineer who will receive a sizable recovery – 20% – for his role in alerting authorities using video surveillance. The flaw not only made it easy for a would-be attacker to access the systems running the devices, but also to hack deeper into those systems after gaining entry.

The key takeaway from all of this is that there is a point of intersection between the whistleblowing system and preventive measures. The whistleblowing system exposes wrongful doings and prevents further complexities arising from such doings.

---

1 *Cisco Settles with Cybersecurity Whistleblower, Setting a Precedent. Available,* CNBC (Jul. 31, 2019), https://www.cnbc.com/2019/07/31/cisco-settles-with-cybersecurity-whistleblower-setting-a-precedent.html.

2.1.2 *Ex Post Tactics*

Now that corruption has already happened, what can be done to confront it? As discussed in the previous section, there are a number of ACAs which belong in the ex post category, namely anti-corruption agencies specialized in law enforcement. This section will mainly focus on post corruption measures. However, some of these agencies also encompass an ex ante role within their onuses, and this will be highlighted. The ex post agencies and measures are listed in the following order: ex post ACAs, other competent authorities (international/inter-governmental level), regulatory environment (international level/ national level), other tools (platforms, initiatives, networks, etc.).

Ex Post ACAs

Anti-corruption agencies can also have law enforcement powers, meaning extra powers and resources, including recourse to elite units dedicated to other internal security challenges like organized crime, terrorism, or espionage, such as New York City's department of investigation.[1] Although the main goal of such agencies is law enforcement (a reactive role), yet there is a preventive aspect to their work. They have prosecutorial authority in corruption cases and sometimes investigative structures and functions too. Examples are the Office Central pour la Répression de la Corruption (OCRC) (Central Office for the Repression of Corruption) in Belgium and the United Kingdom Metropolitan Police/Anti-Corruption Command.

Other Prominent Competent Authorities

From an institutional perspective, the below listed bodies fight corruption on a global and inter-governmental level.

Transparency International (TI) is a non-governmental organization established in 1993, based in Berlin, Germany. Its

1 N.Y.C. Dept. of Investigation, *Inspector General* Unit, NYC. gov, https://www1.nyc.gov/site/doi/offices/inspector-general.page (last visited Dec. 4, 2019).

mission is to abolish corruption and promote transparency, accountability and integrity at all levels and across all sectors of society.[1] TI produces two of the most well-known corruption-related tools: the Corruption Perception Index (CPI) and the Global Corruption Barometer, which will be discussed in section 4 of this chapter. Since corruption is not the same everywhere, TI's community have expanded its anti-corruption scope through a mechanism called TI chapters, whereby countries across the globe can fight corruption via locally established, independent organizations. As chapters are staffed with local experts, they are ideally placed to determine the priorities and approaches best suited to tackling corruption on the ground.[2]

The **World Trade Organization (WTO)** is a global organization founded in 1995, which aims to enable trade to flow as smoothly and freely as possible.[3] As far as anti-corruption efforts are concerned, there are specific parts of WTO's agreements which help to reduce corruption and bad government. One that has a direct impact via the public sector is the Government Procurement Agreement. This agreement disciplines how participating governments make their purchases and opens large sections of procurement markets to foreign competition.[4]

In 1997, when the United Nations Drug Control Program and the Centre for International Crime Prevention merged, the **United Nations Office on Drugs and Crimes (UNODC)**, was created.[5]

1 *Mission, Vision, and Values*, Transparency Int'l, https://www.transparency.org/whoweare/organisation/mission_vision_and_values/0 (last visited Dec. 4, 2019).

2 *Our Chapters*, Transparency Int'l, https://www.transparency.org/whoweare/organisation/our_chapters (last visited Dec. 4, 2019).

3 *The WTO*, World Trade Org. [WTO], https://www.wto.org/english/thewto_e/thewto_e.htm (last visited Dec. 4, 2019).

4 *10 Things the WTO Can Do*, WTO, https://www.wto.org/english/thewto_e/whatis_e/10thi_e/10thi05_e.htm (last visited Dec. 4, 2019).

5 U.N. Office on Drugs and Crime (UNODC), UNHCR Refworld, https://www.refworld.org/publisher,UNODC,,NPL,50ffbce4153,,0.html (last visited Dec. 4, 2019).

It was a global leader in the fight against serious crimes of illicit trafficking, drugs, terrorism and corruption related issues. UNODC fulfills its purpose through three primary functions: firstly, research; secondly, through providing guidance and support for governments in the adoption and implementation of various crime, drugs, terrorism and corruption-related conventions, treaties and protocols; and finally, through offering technical/financial assistance to governments facing challenges in these fields.

As far as corruption is concerned, UNODC seeks to implement the most well-known international anti-corruption convention, the United Nations Convention Against Corruption (UNCAC), through its duty as the secretariat for the Conference of the States Parties (CoSP) to the UNCAC.[1] UNCAC will be explained in detail in forthcoming sections.

In 1961, the **Organization for Economic Co-operation and Development (OECD)**[2] was formed, with the aim of shaping policies which foster prosperity, equality, opportunity and well-being for all. OECD achieves its goals through a unique forum and knowledge hub for data and analysis, exchange of experiences, best practice sharing and advice on public policy and international standard setting.[3]

The OECD's anti-corruption efforts manifested firstly in the OECD Convention on Combating Bribery of Foreign Public Officials in International Business Transactions. Secondly, OECD

---

1 The Conference of the States Parties (COSP) is the main policy-making body of the United Nations Convention against Corruption. It supports states parties and signatories in their implementation of the Convention, and gives policy guidance to UNODC to develop and implement anti-corruption activities. *See Conference of the States Parties to the United Nations Convention against Corruption*, UNODC, https://www.unodc.org/unodc/en/corruption/COSP/conference-of-the-states-parties.html (last visited Nov. 2, 2019).

2 L. De Sousa, *Anti-Corruption Agencies: Between Empowerment and Irrelevance*, 53 Crime, L. & Social Change, no. 1, 2010, at 5, 5-22.

3 *Who We Are*, OECD, https://www.oecd.org/about/ (last visited Nov. 4, 2019).

has a partnership with the Anti-Corruption Working Group (ACWG) of the G20. OECD supports ACWG in fighting foreign bribery, promoting public and private sector integrity, and engaging with the private sector and civil society.

The **Global Organization of Parliamentarians Against Corruption (GOPAC)** is an international, non-governmental alliance, established in 2002 in Canada. It consists of an alliance of legislators working together to combat corruption, strengthen democracy and uphold the rule of law. A unique aspect of GOPAC is that it is the only international network of parliamentarians focused solely on combating corruption, as explicitly mentioned in its vision statement. It aims to: "achieve accountability and transparency through effective anti-corruption mechanisms and inclusive participation and cooperation between parliamentarians, government and civil society".[1] Further, all of GOPAC's core values (integrity, accountability, collaboration, diversity) are related to corruption terminology directly and indirectly.[2] Similarly, in 1999, in Kampala, Uganda, the African Parliamentarians' Network Against Corruption (APNAC) was formed to strengthen the capacity of African parliamentarians to fight corruption and promote good governance. This organization has promoted accountability, transparency and public participation in the processes of government, as the best ways to control corruption.[3]

The **World Bank** is not a bank in the ordinary sense. It was established in 1944 as a unique global partnership between five institutions: the International Bank for Reconstruction and Development

1 *Overview*, Global Org. of Parliaments Against Corruption [GOPAC], http://gopacnetwork.org/overview/ (last visited Nov. 4 2019).

2 *Id.*

3 *What is ANPAC*, African Parliamentarians Network Against Corruption [ANPAC], https://apnacafrica.org/en_US/african-parliamentarians-network-against-corruption/ (last visited Nov. 13, 2019).

(IBRD),[1] the International Development Association (IDA),[2] the International Finance Corporation (IFC),[3] the Multilateral Investment Guarantee Agency (MIGA),[4] and the International

---

1 The International Bank for Reconstruction and Development (IBRD) is a global development cooperative owned by 189 member countries. As the largest development bank in the world, it supports the World Bank Group's mission by providing loans, guarantees, risk management products and advisory services to middle-income and credit-worthy low-income countries, as well as by coordinating responses to regional and global challenges. Created in 1944 to help Europe rebuild after World War II, IBRD joined with IDA, a fund for the poorest countries, to form the World Bank. They work closely with all institutions of the World Bank Group and the public and private sectors in developing countries to reduce poverty and build shared prosperity. *International Bank for Reconstruction and Development*, World Bank, https://www.worldbank.org/en/who-we-are/ibrd (last visited Nov. 13, 2019).

2 The International Development Association (IDA) is the part of the World Bank that helps the world's poorest countries. Overseen by 173 shareholder nations, IDA aims to reduce poverty by providing loans (called "credits") and grants for programs that boost economic growth, reduce inequalities and improve people's living conditions. IDA complements the World Bank's original lending arm — the International Bank for Reconstruction and Development (IBRD). IBRD was established to function as a self-sustaining business and provides loans and advice to middle-income and credit-worthy poor countries. IBRD and IDA share the same staff and headquarters and evaluate projects with the same rigorous standards. *International Development Association*, World Bank, http://ida.worldbank.org/about/what-is-ida (last visited Nov. 18, 2019).

3 Although part of the Bank Group, IFC is a separate legal entity with separate articles of agreement, whilst sharing capital, financial structure, management and staff. Membership of IFC is open only to member countries of the World Bank. *International Finance Corporation*, World Bank, https://www.ifc.org/wps/wcm/connect/corp_ext_content/ifc_external_corporate_site/about+ifc_new/IFC+Governance (last visited Nov. 4, 2019).

4 The Multilateral Investment Guarantee Agency (MIGA) is a member of the World Bank Group. Its mandate is to promote cross-border investment in developing countries by providing guarantees (political risk insurance and credit enhancement) to investors and lenders. MIGA's guarantees protect investments against non-commercial risks and can help investors obtain access to funding sources with improved financial terms and conditions. *About Us*, Multilateral Invest. Guarantee Agency, https://www.miga.org/about-us (last visited Nov. 18, 2019).

Centre for Settlement of Investment Disputes (ICSID).[1] It works for sustainable solutions that reduce poverty and build shared prosperity in developing countries. Although it is a vital source of financial and technical assistance to developing countries around the world, its main role is to reduce poverty and support development, and this justifies its status (not as a bank).

The World Bank confronts corruption and helps foster greater trust and accountability, particularly in environments which are more fragile or suffering from conflict. It leverages innovative technologies to strengthen public sector performance and productivity in order to achieve its goal of reducing corruption. Furthermore, it has adopted a zero-tolerance policy towards corruption. The Bank's approach to fighting corruption combines a preventive (ex ante) policy of anticipating and avoiding risks in its own projects with an ex post approach. It maintains a rigorous scrutiny of projects and works with clients to reduce possible corruption risks that have been identified. This is done through the Bank Group's independent sanctions system, which includes the Integrity Vice Presidency

---

1 ICSID is the world's leading institution devoted to international investment dispute settlement. It has extensive experience in this field, having administered the majority of all international investment cases. States have agreed on ICSID as a forum for investor-state dispute settlement in most international investment treaties and in numerous investment laws and contracts. ICSID was established in 1966 by the Convention on the Settlement of Investment Disputes between States and Nationals of Other States (the ICSID Convention). The ICSID Convention is a multilateral treaty formulated by the Executive Directors of the World Bank to further the Bank's objective of promoting international investment. ICSID is an independent, depoliticized and effective dispute-settlement institution. Its availability to investors and states helps to promote international investment by providing confidence in the dispute resolution process. It is also available for state-state disputes under investment treaties and free trade agreements, and as an administrative registry, *International Centre for Settlement of Investment Disputes*, World Bank, https://icsid.worldbank.org/en/Pages/about/default.aspx (last visited Nov. 18, 2019).

(INT) unit[1] responsible for investigating allegations of fraud and corruption in World Bank-funded projects. Public complaint mechanisms are built into projects to encourage and empower oversight, and projects are actively supervised during implementation.[2]

The **International Group for Anti-Corruption Coordination (IGAC)** is coordinated by the United Nations Office on Drugs and Crime and is composed of international organizations active in the field of anti-corruption, including several United Nations agencies, the World Bank, the Asian Development Bank (ADB) and other regional development banks, the Organization for Economic Co-operation and Development (OECD), the European Union and the Council of Europe, besides several international non-governmental organizations.[3]

The primary mission of the **International Criminal Police Organization (INTERPOL)** is law enforcement. INTERPOL is an inter-governmental organization which supports police forces around the world to create a safer world. It enables them to share and access data on crimes and criminals, offering a range of technical and operational support, including investigative support such as forensics, analysis and assistance in locating fugitives around the world. Moreover, as crime evolves, INTERPOL keeps an eye on the future through research into international crime and trends.[4]

Corruption is part of INTERPOL's scope in combating organized crime.[5] It works with law enforcement, legal experts, the banking

1 *Integrity Vice Presidency*, World Bank, https://www.worldbank.org/en/about/unit/integrity-vice-presidency (last visited Dec. 2, 2019).

2 *Combating Corruption*, World Bank, https://www.worldbank.org/en/topic/governance/brief/anti-corruption (last visited Dec. 2, 2019).

3 Press Release, U.N. Info. Serv., International Anti-Corruption Coordination Group Discusses Preventing and Controlling Corruption in Emergency Disaster Relief. April, U.N. Press Release BKK/CP/21 (Apr. 23, 2005).
What is INTEROPL, Int'l Crim. Police Org., https://www.interpol.int/en/Who-we-are/What-is-INTERPOL (last visited Dec. 2, 2019).

4 *What is INTEROPL*, Int'l Crim. Police Org., https://www.interpol.int/en/Who-we-are/What-is-INTERPOL (last visited Dec. 2, 2019).

5 Definition of Organized Crime: shall mean a structured group of three or more

sector and all affected industries to detect stolen assets, stop their movement across borders and prevent corruption. INTERPOL's global policing capabilities, which include eighteen global databases and a global communication system, enable the secure sharing of details such as financial information and online activities. Specialized networks such as the INTERPOL/StAR Global Focal Point Platform on Asset Recovery[1] and the Match Fixing Task Force[2] complement its range of capabilities. This all showcases INTERPOL's significant role in the job of fighting corruption.

Established in 2003, the **Basel Institute on Governance** is a non-profit Swiss foundation dedicated to working with public and private partners around the world to strengthen governance and prevent and combat corruption and other financial crimes.[3] Addressing corruption through leveling competitors and raising

---

persons, existing for a period of time and acting in concert with the aim of committing one or more serious crimes or offences established in accordance with this Convention, in order to obtain, directly or indirectly, a financial or other material benefit. *See* U.N. Convention on Transnational and Organized Crime and the Protocols Thereto (2004), https://www.unodc.org/documents/treaties/UNTOC/Publications/TOC%20Convention/TOCebook-e.pdf [hereinafter Convention on Transnational and Organized Crime].

1 StAR Global Focal Point Platform on Asset Recovery. This is a joint Interpol-StAR (Stolen Asset Recovery) initiative to establish a platform that can be used by practitioners appointed by their government to exchange operational information. *The Global Focal Point Conference*, World Bank, https://star.worldbank.org/events?keys=&sort_by=score&sort_order=DESC&items_per_page=10 (last visited Nov. 2, 2019).

2 Match Fixing Taskforce (IMFTF). IMFTF was created in 2011 to support member countries with investigations and law enforcement operations in all sports, and maintain a global network of investigators for the sharing of information, intelligence and best practices. *INTERPOL Match Fixing Task Force Closes Ranks on Organized Crime*, INTERPOL (Sept. 12, 2018), https://www.interpol.int/es/Noticias-y-acontecimientos/Noticias/2018/INTERPOL-Match-Fixing-Task-Force-closes-ranks-on-organized-crime.

3 *About Us*, Basel Inst. on Governance, https://www.baselgovernance.org/about-us (last visited Nov. 18, 2019).

business integrity is an innovative approach adopted by the **International Centre for Collective Action (ICCA)**.

ICCA is an independent center of excellence in anti-corruption collective action. It develops and facilitates collective action initiatives that bring together businesses and other stakeholders to solve problems of corruption in industries worldwide.[1]

Regulatory Environment (International Level)

On the international legal level, corruption is either explicitly regulated in standalone laws issued solely to deal with it, or implicitly through various types of laws against organized crime, transitional crime, FATF, etc. The same applies nationally, with standalone laws explicitly countering corruption, or implicitly, through civil, criminal and anti-money laundering (AML) laws. Below is a list of examples to clarify the difference between the two.

Explicit anti-corruption regulations. The **United Nations Convention against Corruption (UNCAC)** is the only global legal instrument that explicitly addresses corruption as its main target. This Convention was drafted and signed in 2003 and came into force in 2005.[2] The United Nations Office on Drugs and Crimes (UNODC) serves as its secretariat. It consists of eight chapters. The five major pillars of the UNCAC are summed up in preventive measures, criminalization and law enforcement, international cooperation, asset recovery, and technical assistance and information exchange. As observed from the listed components, the UNCAC combines both ex ante and ex poste approaches.

In the UNCAC, various forms of corruption are detected and defined, including bribery, embezzlement, trading in influence, abuse of functions, obstruction of justice and money laundering. The

1 *International Centre for Collective Action*, Basel Inst. on Governance, https://www.baselgovernance.org/collective-action (last visited Nov. 18, 2019).

2 See generally UNCAC.

UNCAC covers corruption offenses in both public and private sectors. It is the only legally binding *universal* anti-corruption instrument. In a later section, the UNCAC and its individual articles will be analyzed and discussed in detail.

The **Arab Convention on Anti-Corruption** aims at uncovering and addressing all forms of corruption and other offences related to its commission, and facilitating prosecution of its perpetrators. It also fosters integrity, transparency, accountability and the rule of law, encouraging individuals and civil society organizations to take an active part in preventing and fighting corruption.[1] The Arab Convention on Anti-Corruption consists of thirty-five articles, covering thirteen corruption offenses, as follows: 1) bribery of a public official, 2) bribery in public sector companies, joint-stock companies, associations and institutions linked with the public interest, 3) bribery in the private sector, 4) bribery of foreign public officials and officials of public international organizations in connection with international trade within a state party, 5) influence peddling, 6) abuse of public office, 7) illicit enrichment, 8) laundering of the proceeds of crime, 9) concealing the proceeds of crime obtained from the acts stipulated in the present article, 10) obstructing the course of justice, 11) misappropriation of public property and its unlawful acquisition, 12) misappropriation of the property of joint-stock companies, public-interest private associations and in the private sector, 13) participation in or attempt to commit the offences stipulated in the present article.[2]

This Convention also adopts an ex ante approach, as shown in article 10, which lays down measures for prevention of corruption; and in article 11, which regulates civil society participation, specifically encouraging effective participation by civil society organizations in raising social awareness about the fight against corruption, its causes and seriousness and the threat it represents to the interests of society at large. Article 11 also supports the conducting of media

1 Arab Anti-Corruption Convention (2010).

2 *Id.* art. 4.

campaigns against corruption, as well as awareness programs, including developing material for school and university curricula.

Needless to say, the Convention also provides for ex post action in many ways, such as its sanctions for acts of corruption in article 13[1] and provision of victim support in article 15.[2]

The **African Union Convention on Preventing and Combating Corruption (AUCPCC)** was signed in 2003 and came into force in 2006.[3] It consists of twenty-eight articles and is wide enough to cover a range of corruption offenses in both private and public sectors. Example of such offenses include bribery (domestic or foreign), diversion of property by public officials, trading in influence, illicit enrichment, money laundering and concealment of property. It primarily consists of mandatory provisions. AUCPCC regulates a number of important issues, such as minimum guarantees for fair trial, in accordance with the African Human Rights Charter and relevant international human rights instruments. An example of an issue related to corruption is bank secrecy. The AUCPCC does not permit countries to invoke banking secrecy to justify their refusal to cooperate, with regard to acts of corruption and related offenses.[4]

The **Council of Europe Corruption Laws** tackled

---

1 *Id.* art. 13. "While giving due consideration to the rights acquired by bona fide third parties, each State Party shall, in accordance with its domestic legislation, adopt measures to punish corruption. In this context, State Parties may take corruption into consideration as an important factor when taking legal steps to cancel or revoke a contract, withdraw a concession or other similar arrangements, or taking any other remedial measure".

2 *Id.* art. 15. Arab Anti-Corruption Convention, Article 15. "1. Each State Party shall lay down appropriate procedural rules to provide victims of the offences included in the present Convention with the means to obtain compensation and remedy. 2. Each State Party shall give, subject to its domestic legislation, the chance for victims to air their views and for those views to be taken into account at the appropriate stages of the criminal proceedings instituted against offenders, without prejudice to the rights of the defense".

3 African Union Convention on Preventing and Combating Corruption (2003).

4 *Id.* art. 17.

corruption in Europe using a three-pronged approach, comprising common standards, monitoring mechanisms and assistance projects.[1] Standards are developed through conventions, resolutions and recommendations. Monitoring mechanisms consist of the following: 1. GRECO,[2] 2. MONEYVAL,[3] and 3. COP 198.[4, 5] Assistance activities come in the form of programs, projects and activities. In this section, two major aspects will be discussed: criminal discourse

---

1 Council of Europe, Action Against Economic Crime (Nov. 4, 2015), *available at* https://www.unodc.org/documents/treaties/UNCAC/COSP/session6/Special-Events/2015_11_03_GuillaumaParentCouncelofEurope.pdf.

2 GRECO is the Group of States Against Corruption, a group that aims to: 1. monitor compliance with the Council of Europe's anti-corruption standards. 2. identify deficiencies and prompt reforms. 3. promote and share good practices. This group follows an evaluation procedure, as follows: 1. evaluation rounds based on a specific theme. 2. questionnaire and on-site visit. 3. country-specific evaluation report. 4. publication of the report. 4. compliance procedure and publication of its results. *Id.*

3 MONEYVAL is the Committee of Experts on the Evaluation of Anti-Money Laundering Measures and the Financing of Terrorism. Its objectives are to: 1. monitor compliance with AML/CFT international standards (FATF and 3rd EU directive). 2. identify deficiencies, provide recommendations and share good practices. 3. identify ML/TF typologies, trends, techniques. It follows a certain evaluation procedure: 1. evaluation rounds every 5-7 years. 2. questionnaire and on-site visit. 3. country-specific evaluation report and its publication. 4. compliance assessment and publication of its results. *Id.*

4 COP 198 is the 2005 Convention on Laundering, Search, Seizure and Confiscation of the Proceeds from Crime and on the Financing of Terrorism (CETS 198). This convention provides states with enhanced possibilities to prosecute money laundering more effectively. It further equips states parties with more confiscation tools to deprive offenders of criminal proceeds, and provides important investigative powers, including measures to access banking information for domestic investigations and for the purposes of international co-operation. The Convention also covers preventive measures, the role and responsibilities of financial intelligence units and the principles for international co-operation between them. Finally, it applies all its provisions to financing of terrorism and covers the principles on which judicial international co-operation should operate between contracting state parties. *About COP*, Council of Europe, https://www.coe.int/en/web/cop198/about-cop (last visited October 10, 2019).

5 Council of Europe, *supra* note 207.

(Criminal Law Convention on Corruption) and civil discourse (Civil Law Convention on Corruption).

The **Criminal Law Convention on Corruption (CETS 173),** issued in 1999, is wide-ranging in scope and complements existing legal instruments. This forty-two article Convention provides for complementary criminal law measures, improved international co-operation in the prosecution of corruption offences, all monitored by the Group of States against Corruption (GRECO). CETS 173 is similar to UNCAC in terms of the setting up of specialized anti-corruption bodies, protection of persons collaborating with investigating or prosecuting authorities, gathering of evidence and confiscation of proceeds. It mirrors UNCAC also in providing for enhanced international co-operation (mutual assistance, extradition and the provision of information) in the investigation and prosecution of corruption offences.[1] The Convention covers many forms of corruption, as listed below:[2]

- Active and passive bribery of domestic and foreign public officials.
- Active and passive bribery of national and foreign parliamentarians and of members of international parliamentary assemblies.
- Active and passive bribery in the private sector.
- Active and passive bribery of international civil servants.
- Active and passive bribery of domestic, foreign and international judges and officials of international courts.
- Active and passive trading in influence.
- Money laundering of proceeds from corruption offences.
- Accounting offences (invoices, accounting documents, etc.) connected with corruption offences.

---

1 Criminal Law Convention on Corruption, *supra* note 110.

2 Council of Europe, *supra* note 207.

The **Civil Law Convention on Corruption (CETS 174)** was the first attempt to define common international rules in the field of civil law and corruption. It was issued in 1999 and consists of three chapters: measures to be taken at the national level, international co-operation, and monitoring of implementation and final clauses. As far as the civil law component is concerned, the Convention mandates compensation for damages caused by corruption offenses and the protection of employees who report corruption. It regulates for contributory negligence, including reduction or disallowance of compensation, depending on the circumstances. The validity of contracts is a notable aspect of the Convention, which requires clarity and accuracy of accounts, audits and acquisition of evidence. It goes without saying that liability is a major issue (including state liability for acts of corruption committed by public officials). Sanctions wise, court orders preserve the assets necessary for execution of the final judgment and the maintenance of the *status quo*, pending resolution of the points at issue. Similarly, as in CETS 173 (GRECO), commitments entered into under the Convention by the state party will be monitored.[1]

The **OECD Anti-Bribery Convention**, also known as OECD, is the first and only international anti-corruption instrument focused on the 'supply side' of the bribery transaction.[2] It promotes a bribe-free, level playing field for companies around the world.[3] The Convention's notable effect in reducing political corruption and corporate crime is due to its sanctions against bribery

1 Civil Law Convention on Corruption, E.T.S. 174 (Jan. 11, 2003).

2 OECD, Directorate for Financial and Enterprise Affairs Working Group on Bribery in International Business Transactions Review of the 2009 Anti-Bribery Recommendation 4 (2019), http://www.oecd.org/officialdocuments/publicdisplaydocumentpdf/?cote=DAF/WGB(2018)56/FINAL&docLanguage=En.

3 Strengthening Enforcement of the OECD Anti-Bribery Convention, Transparency Int'l, https://www.transparency.org/whatwedo/activity/strengthening_enforcement_of_the_oecd_anti_bribery_convention (last visited Nov. 2, 2019).

in international business transactions carried out by companies based in the Convention member countries. It has established legally binding standards to criminalize bribery of foreign public officials in such transactions and provides for a host of related measures which make this effective.[1] Although the Convention is mainly focused on combating bribery, through criminalizing the offering or giving of bribes (but not of soliciting or receiving bribes), it also addresses other offenses, such as money laundering. OECD Anti-Bribery Convention signatories are required to put in place legislation that criminalizes the act of bribing a foreign public official. Working groups on bribery are formed to monitor the implementation of the Convention, since OECD has no authority to implement it.

In 1977, the **Foreign Corrupt Practices Act (FCPA)** was enacted for the purpose of making it unlawful for certain classes of persons and entities to make payments to foreign government officials, to help obtain or retain business.[2] The FCPA can apply to prohibited conduct anywhere in the world and extends to publicly traded companies and their officers, directors, employees, stockholders and agents. Agents can include third party agents, consultants, distributors, joint-venture partners and others.[3] It is worth noting that the U.S. Securities and Exchange Commission (SEC) and the Department of Justice (DOJ) have charged hundreds of companies and individuals with FCPA violations and imposed billions of dollars in monetary sanctions since the statute's enactment in 1977. U.S. authorities have intensified their efforts to reduce corruption by increasing personnel, collaborating more closely with foreign

---

1 Convention on Combating Bribery of Foreign Public Officials (Nov. 21, 1997).

2 *Foreign Corrupt Practices Act – Overview*, U.S. Dept. of Justice, https://www.justice.gov/criminal-fraud/foreign-corrupt-practices-act (last visited Oct. 10, 2019).

3 Spotlight on Foreign Corrupt Practices Act, U.S. Securities & Exchange Comm'n, https://www.sec.gov/spotlight/foreign-corrupt-practices-act.shtml (last visited Nov. 4, 2019).

governments and agencies, and offering mitigation credit to companies that self-disclose FCPA violations and cooperate with the government's investigation. In addition, there is a clearing house called the Foreign Corrupt Practices Act Clearinghouse (FCPAC), which operates as a database, a repository of original source documents and a supplier of analytics, providing users with detailed information relating to enforcement of the Foreign Corrupt Practices Act (FCPA). This clearing house provides investors, policymakers, scholars, judges, lawyers, the media and the public at large with a comprehensive website for all things FCPA-related. Users can review relevant laws, read articles about FCPA compliance and enforcement, and view, search and sort data about FCPA investigations and enforcement actions, according to their individual needs and interests.[1] It provides the most up-to-date information on trends in FCPA investigations and academic literature.

Implicit anti-corruption regulations. As a reminder, implicit here means that the legal instrument addresses corruption indirectly. It tackles corruption without mentioning the word.

In 2000, the United Nations issued the **Convention against Transnational Organized Crime (UNTOC)**, also known as the Palermo convention. This Convention is operated and supervised by the United Nations Office of Drugs and Crimes (UNODC). A collection of three main protocols supplements UNTOC: 1) the Protocol to Prevent, Suppress and Punish Trafficking in Persons, Especially Women and Children,[2] 2) the Protocol against the Smuggling of

1 Foreign Corrupt Practices Act Clearing House, Stanford Law School, http://fcpa.stanford.edu/ (last visited Nov. 2, 2019).

2 U.N. Hum. Rts. Off. of the High Comm'r [OHCHR], Protocol to Prevent, Suppress and Punish Trafficking in Persons Especially Women and Children, supplementing the United Nations Convention against Transnational Organized Crime (2000), https://www.ohchr.org/en/professionalinterest/pages/protocoltraffickinginpersons.

Migrants by Land, Sea and Air,[1] and 3) the Protocol against the Illicit Manufacturing of and Trafficking in Firearms.[2] As stated in the general provisions of these protocols, they supplement the United Nations Convention against Transnational Organized Crime.

The special connection between the UNTOC and corruption has been addressed on several occasions by the United Nations itself and academia. From the United Nations' point of view, there is clear cross-referencing between the main corruption convention (UNCAC) and UNTOC. In article 8, UNTOC called for the criminalization of corruption,[3] clearly referencing the term, and it elaborated further on one of its most well-known forms, i.e. bribery in the public sector. Article 9 also endorsed the adoption of measures to tackle corruption.[4] There is also a perceived link between corruption and organized crime, which prompted the UN General Assembly to adopt Resolution 55/61 in December of 2000, recognizing that an international legal document against corruption, independent of the Convention against Transnational Organized Crime, was necessary.

On the other hand, in its preamble section, UNCAC declared to the states which were party to the Convention that it was: "concerned

---

1 UNTOC, Protocol against the Smuggling of Migrants by Land, Sea and Air, supplementing the United Nations Convention against Transnational Organized Crime (2000), https://www.unodc.org/documents/middleeastandnorthafrica/smuggling-migrants/SoM_Protocol_English.pdf.

2 G.A. Res. 55/255, UN Protocol against the Illicit Manufacturing and Trafficking in Firearms (Jun. 8, 2001).

3 Convention against Transnational and Organized Crime, *supra* note 195, at art. 8.

4 Article 9 1. In addition to the measures set forth in article 8 of this Convention, each State Party shall, to the extent appropriate and consistent with its legal system, adopt legislative, administrative or other effective measures to promote integrity and to prevent, detect and punish the corruption of public officials. *Id.* art. 9.

2. Each State Party shall take measures to ensure effective action by its authorities in the prevention, detection and punishment of the corruption of public officials, including providing such authorities with adequate independence to deter the exertion of inappropriate influence on their action. *Id.* at 10-11.

also about the links between corruption and other forms of crime, in particular organized crime and economic crime, including money-laundering" and that it was "convinced that corruption is no longer a local matter but a transnational phenomenon that affects all societies and economies, making international cooperation to prevent and control it essential".[1] Just as UNTOC did, UNCAC made a clear reference to the terms "organized crimes" and "transitional". In 1994, the United Nations' Naples Declaration officially recognized that organized crime has a "corrupting influence on fundamental social, economic and political institutions" and that the common practice of organized criminal networks is to use "violence, intimidation and corruption to earn profit or control territories or markets".[2]

Additionally, the Council of Europe acknowledged the existence of links between corruption and organized crime. One of the Twenty Guiding Principles for the Fight against Corruption (adopted in 1997) seeks "to ensure that in every aspect of the fight against corruption, the possible connections with organized crime and money laundering are taken into account".[3]

Numerous academics and scholars have argued that corruption and organized crime are conjoined twins. For instance: "Definitions of organized crime often include corruption as central to it, largely because of the commercial benefits of ensuring a smooth supply of vice".[4,5] Also:

---

1 *Id.*

2 G.A. Res. 49/159, Naples Political Declaration and Global Action against Organized Transnational Crime (Dec. 23, 1994); G.A. Res. 1996/27, Implementation of the Naples Political Declaration and Global Action Plan against Organized Transnational Crime (Jul. 24, 1996).

3 Council of Europe Res. (97)24 on the 20 Guiding Principles for the Fight against Corruption (Jun. 11, 1997).

4 James O. Finckenauer, *Problems of Definition: What is Organized Crime?* 8 Trends Organ. Crim. 56, 63-83 (2005).

5 F.E. Hagan, *"Organized Crime" and "Organized Crime": Indeterminate Problems of Definition*, 9 Trends Organ. Crim. 129 (2006).

Corruption is often intertwined with international organized crime and is facilitated by money laundering. Self-reinforcing spirals of corruption occur when organized crime infiltrates state institutions. Criminal activity may become so intertwined with corrupt politics and legitimate business, that it is difficult to tell them apart.[1]

There are even specialized nonprofit organizations such as the **Organized Crimes and Corruption Reporting Projects (OCCRP)** which work to turn the tables on corruption and build greater accountability, through exposing the abuse of power at the expense of the people. OCCRP serves people whose lives are affected by organized crime and corruption. It is committed to transnational investigative reporting and promotes technology-based approaches to exposing organized crime and corruption worldwide.[2]

Corruption and organized crime are closely related and one leads to another. And whenever corruption is present, organized crime may have a stake in the profits.

The **Financial Action Task Force (FATF)** is an independent inter-governmental organization, established in 1989. FATF Recommendations are recognized as global anti-money laundering (AML) and counter-terrorist financing (CFT) standards. The FATF is therefore a "policy-making body" which works to generate the necessary political will to bring about national legislative and regulatory reforms in these areas. It attaches great importance to the fight against corruption. In its view, corruption has the potential to severely damage economic development, frustrate the fight against organized crime, and weaken respect for the law and effective

1 Kaushik Basu & Tito Cordella, *Institutions, Governance and the Control of Corruption*, 157 IEA Conference, 2018, at 75-111.

2 *Who We Are*, Org. Crime &Corruption Reporting Project [OCCRP], https://www.occrp.org/en/about-us (last visited Oct. 4, 2019).

governance.[1] The FATF further works to identify national-level vulnerabilities, with the aim of protecting the international financial system from misuse. 'Misuse' is generally defined as an illegal, corrupt act; and although the focus of the FATF Recommendations is on combating money laundering and terrorist financing, they include specific measures which recognize corruption risks as well. Examples of these measures are requiring countries to make corruption and bribery predicate offences for money laundering, requiring financial institutions to take action to mitigate the risks posed by politically exposed persons (PEPs), requiring countries to have mechanisms in place to recover (through confiscation) the proceeds of crime, and requiring countries to implement the UNCAC.

Corruption and money laundering are intrinsically linked. Corruption offences, such as bribery or theft of public funds, are generally committed for the sake of private gain. Money laundering is the process of concealing illicit gains generated from criminal activity. The G20 called upon the FATF to address the problem of corruption in the framework of its work on combating money laundering and terrorist financing. The G20 is an international economic cooperation forum which brings together the leaders of both developed and developing countries from every continent, representing around 80% of the world's economic output, two-thirds of the global population and three-quarters of international trade.[2]

The FATF publication, 'Best Practices Paper: The Use of the FATF Recommendations to Combat Corruption', defines 'the proceeds' as funds involved in (the instruments of crime) and the proceeds derived or generated from corruption offences.[3] The

1 Financial Action Task Force [FATF], The Use of the FATF Recommendations to Combat Corruption 5 Oct. 2013), http://www.fatf-gafi.org/media/fatf/documents/recommendations/BPP-Use-of-FATF-Recs-Corruption.pdf.

2 *What is G20?* G20, https://g20.org/en/about/Pages/whatis.aspx, (last visited Oct. 4, 2019).

3 FATF, *supra* note 233, at 5.

FATF Recommendations were designed to combat money laundering and terrorist financing, but when effectively implemented they can also help combat corruption, by safeguarding the integrity of the public sector, protecting designated private sector institutions from abuse, increasing transparency of the financial system, facilitating the detection, investigation and prosecution of those involved in corruption and money laundering, and aiding in the recovery of stolen assets.[1] In summary, the FATF addresses forms of corruption that are linked to financial proceeds.

It is 2020 already and the current epoch is fast, virtual and borderless, which highlights the need for cybercrime regulations. The **Anti-Corruption Research Education Center (ACREC)** has offered a definition of cybercrime which links cybercrime and corruption and provides an approach to what is happening on the ground. This definition highlights that cybercrime is not just a virus found on your computer. Corrupt officials have learned how to use the latest information technology for money laundering.[2] Now corruption has become a silent crime, harder to trace and detect. Cyber space was created to better serve humanity and facilitate business dealings around the world, but alongside its development, there has been a directly proportional increase in massive destructive effects caused by cybercrime, which result in billions of dollars in losses for rights holders and legitimate businesses around the world.

The link between cybercrime and corruption can manifest in countless shapes and forms. UNCAC's article 48 (3) referenced modern technology in the following: "State Parties shall endeavor to cooperate within their means to respond to offences covered by this Convention committed through the use of modern technology".[3]

---

1 *Id.*

2 *Corruption and Cybercrimes Double Challenge for Investment*, Anti-Corruption Res. Educ. Center [ACREC], https://acrec.org.ua/en/events/corruption-and-cybercrimes-double-challenge-for-investments/ (last visited Nov. 4, 2019).

3 *See generally* UNCAC.

These offenses include, for example, computer crimes or cybercrimes enabling corruption offenses, or the use of computers to commit such crimes. In 2015, INTERPOL opened a global complex for innovation on cybercrime in Singapore, reacting to the fact that criminals are increasingly taking advantage of new technology.[1]

It is important to be aware of the fact that cyber space is a greased and expanding wheel of corruption due to its fast and accessible nature. Cyber crooks exploit every opportunity they find, quickly embracing new strategies for attacking companies. Long-established transnational organized crime groups are also constantly finding new ways to use technology to facilitate traditional forms of crime, for example using virtual currencies and the deep web to create illicit global markets.[2] On a larger scale, funding of transnational organized crime networks which trade in counterfeit and pirated products also provides criminals with the means to bribe and corrupt the rule of law. Further, cyber corruption is gaining momentum and emerging technologies may reshape the landscape of anti-corruption in the future.

Public procurement laws aim to protect a section of government which is extremely vulnerable to corruption. Corruption in this field is not just about money. It also reduces the quality of work or services. And it can cost lives. People in many countries have paid a terrible personal price for collapsed buildings and counterfeit medicines.[3] One might wonder why procurement laws are an important component in the implicit international instruments fighting corruption. This is because procurement spending may represent 10-20% of GDP and up to 50% or even more of total government spending. The nature of procurement necessarily involves a risk of abuse, and the

---

1 Cecily Rose et al., The United Nations Convention Against Corruption: A Commentary ch. 3 (2019).

2 *Cybercrime and Intellectual Property Crime*, U.S. Dep. of State, https://www.state.gov/cybercrime-and-intellectual-property-crime/ (last visited Oct. 4, 2019).

3 *Public Procurement*, Transparency Int'l, https://www.transparency.org/topic/detail/public_procurement (last visited Nov. 4, 2019).

size of the market shows that potential losses could be significant, but also procurement involves important projects (health, education, infrastructure), which will have a major impact on economic performance and development. Accordingly, achieving value for money in procurement is critical. Responding to these key factors, the UNCITRAL Model Law on International Commercial Arbitration allows the enacting state to develop a procurement system that will achieve value for money and avoid abuse.[1] One of the clauses in the United Nations Commission on International Trade Law states that:

> *the UNCITRAL Model Law has also been prepared with a view to supporting the harmonization of international standards in public procurement, and takes account of the UN Convention Against Corruption, the Procurement Guidelines and Consultant Guidelines of the World Bank and the equivalent documents of other IFIs.*

Therefore, the link is recognized internationally.[2] Furthermore, it is alluded to in UNCITRAL's preamble, as follows:

> *(d) Providing for the fair, equal and equitable treatment of all suppliers and contractors; (e) Promoting the integrity of, and fairness and public confidence in, the procurement process; (f) Achieving transparency in the procedures relating to procurement.*[3]

Corruption still lingers. Integrity and transparency are both positive projections of anti-corruption. This was highlighted in the

1 *UNCITRAL Model Law on Public Procurement*, UNCITRAL (2011), https://uncitral.un.org/en/texts/procurement/modellaw/public_procurement.

2 *Id.*

3 UNCITRAL Model Law on Public Procurement 3 (2011), *available at* https://uncitral.un.org/sites/uncitral.un.org/files/media-documents/uncitral/en/2011-model-law-on-public-procurement-e.pdf.

statement on the pernicious impact of corruption on trade and development made by the UNODC executive director at an event celebrating the 50th Anniversary of UNCITRAL.[1] In addition to the volume of transactions and the financial interests at stake, corruption risks are exacerbated by the complexity of the process, the close interaction between public officials and businesses, and the multitude of stakeholders.[2] Therefore, from a pure anti-corruption perspective, procurement has its fair share of concern. In the UNCAC particularly, in chapter 2, preventive measures relevant to procurement are explicitly mentioned in 'Procurement Measures and Management of Public Finances' (Article 9),[3] and implicitly

1 Press Release, UNDOC Executive Director Statement on the Pernicious Impact of Corruption on Trade and Development (July 4, 2017), https://www.unodc.org/unodc/en/press/releases/2017/July/statement-on-the-pernicious-impact-of-corruption-on-trade-and-development-at-event-celebrating-the-50th-anniversary-of-uncitral.html.

2 OECD, Preventing Corruption in Public Procurement 6 (2016), http://www.oecd.org/gov/ethics/Corruption-Public-Procurement-Brochure.pdf.

3 Public procurement and management of public finances.
1. Each State Party shall, in accordance with the fundamental principles of its legal system, take the necessary steps to establish appropriate systems of procurement, based on transparency, competition and objective criteria in decision-making, that are effective, inter alia, in preventing corruption. Such systems, which may take into account appropriate threshold values in their application, shall address, inter alia: (a) The public distribution of information relating to procurement procedures and contracts, including information on invitations to tender and relevant or pertinent information on the award of contracts, allowing potential tenderers sufficient time to prepare and submit their tenders; (b) The establishment, in advance, of conditions for participation, including selection and award criteria and tendering rules, and their publication; (c) The use of objective and predetermined criteria for public procurement decisions, in order to facilitate the subsequent verification of the correct application of the rules or procedures; (d) An effective system of domestic review, including an effective system of appeal, to ensure legal recourse and remedies in the event that the rules or procedures established pursuant to this paragraph are not followed; (e) Where appropriate, measures to regulate matters regarding personnel responsible for procurement, such as declaration of interest in particular public procurements, screening procedures and training requirements.

referenced in 'Transparency in Public Administration' (Article 10)[1] and Codes of Conduct (Article 8).[2] These measures support and fortify a robust procurement system and prove that it is an influential component of the anti-corruption system. Although regulations are in place and are constantly being updated, corruption can still arise in various forms during each phase of the procurement process. Almost two-thirds of the foreign bribery cases studied occurred in sectors closely associated with contracts or licensing through public procurement: extraction, construction, transportation and storage, and the information and communication sectors.[3] Whether it is the WTO Government Procurement Agreement (GPA)[4] or the

---

2. Each State Party shall, in accordance with the fundamental principles of its legal system, take appropriate measures to promote transparency and accountability in the management of public finances. Such measures shall encompass, inter alia: (a) Procedures for the adoption of the national budget; (b) Timely reporting on revenue and expenditure; (c) A system of accounting and auditing standards and related oversight; (d) Effective and efficient systems of risk management and internal control; and (e) Where appropriate, corrective action in the case of failure to comply with the requirements established in this paragraph.

3. Each State Party shall take such civil and administrative measures as may be necessary, in accordance with the fundamental principles of its domestic law, to preserve the integrity of accounting books, records, financial statements or other documents related to public expenditure and revenue and to prevent the falsification of such documents. *See* UNCAC.

1 *Id.*

2 *Id.*

3 OECD, Foreign Bribery Report (2014), http://dx.doi.org/10.1787/9789264226616-en.

4 Model WTO GPA law, now in a revised version adopted in 2012, and in force since 2014. GPA applies only to large contracts above specified threshold values. It is what is known as a plurilateral agreement which has been signed by a majority of states but by no means all WTO members. It sets out minimum requirements on transparent, non-discriminatory contract awards and provides for protection under procurement law. Peter Schäfer, ***Public Procurement – European and International Law Governing Public Procurement***, BDI (2016), https://english.bdi.eu/article/news/public-procurement-european-and-international-law-governing-public-procurement/.

UNCITRAL,[1] various types of corrupt practices may exploit these vulnerabilities, such as embezzlement, undue influence in the needs assessment, bribery of public officials involved in the award process, or fraud in bid evaluations, invoices or contract obligations. Corruption infects budgeting, soliciting and awarding. Other corrupt practices include falsely reporting damaged equipment in order to create an excess supply that could be used for corrupt purposes, or setting budgets artificially high, so that excess allocations can be stolen or diverted. Accepting late proposals or rejecting legitimate proposals are further examples.[2]

Thus it can be seen that procurement law is a key factor in creating a healthy environment free from corruption.

Regulatory Environment (National Level)

On the national level, anti-corruption matters are either explicitly regulated in a standalone law, as in the anti-corruption laws in the United States,[3] Belize,[4] Kuwait,[5] Algeria,[6]

1 UNCITRAL Model Law on Public Procurement with its accompanying Guide to Enactment of the UNCITRAL Model Law on Public Procurement has been created as an encouragement for states which want to create new public procurement rules or reform existing ones. *Id.*

2 Jason P. Matechak, *Fighting Corruption in Public Procurement*, Center for Int'l Private Enterprise (CIPE), https://www.cipe.org/legacy/publication-docs/matechak.pdf (last visited Nov. 4, 2019).

3 The United States promulgated the Anti-Corruption Act; the text of the law is available at: Represent.Us, The American Anti-Corruption Act Constitutionality (2013), *available at* https://web.archive.org/web/20190614214447/https://s3.amazonaws.com/s3.unitedrepublic.org/docs/AACA_Constitutionality.pdf.

4 The Belize Prevention of Corruption Act (2007), *available at* https://publicofficialsfinancialdisclosure.worldbank.org/sites/fdl/files/assets/law-library-files/Belize_Anti-Corruption%20Law_2007_en.pdf.

5 The Kuwait Anti-Corruption Authority Establishment and Financial Disclosure Provisions Law (2016), *available at* http://nazaha.ps/wp-content/uploads/2019/01/قانون-مكافحة-الفساد-الكويتي.pdf.

6 Algeria Anti-Corruption Legislation, Law No. 06-01 of 21 on the Prevention and the Fight Against Corruption (Feb. 20, 2006).

India,[1] Lebanon,[2] Palestine[3] and Kenya,[4] meaning that the titles of the laws explicitly include the word corruption. Or such matters can be dealt with in various laws that in their turn either mention the word corruption explicitly in their text or regulate forms of corruption offenses. These laws include penal codes, money laundering laws and acts against bribery. Examples of different legal scenarios will be provided below.

Explicit laws and regulations. These are cases of laws which are focused entirely on anti-corruption and their titles include the word corruption. When corruption is explicitly regulated in a standalone law, such laws provide a framework for a broad range of preventive and enforcement measures, and in some cases, for the establishment of special anti-corruption agencies. They often provide for whistleblower protection and require public servants to disclose their income and assets. Apart from defining and prohibiting different forms of corruption, anti-corruption legislation also usually outlines specific rules of evidence that can be used to facilitate investigation and pressing of corruption charges, and they specify the powers of the institutions and officials in charge of implementation of the anti-corruption law.[5]

The Prevention of Corruption Act 1988, which was passed in

---

1 The India Corruption Act 1988 (and as amended 2003), *available at* http://legislative.gov.in/sites/default/files/A1988-49.pdf (1988) and https://www.prsindia.org/sites/default/files/bill_files/1376983957~~PCA_Bill_2013_0.pdf (2013).

2 The Lebanon Anti-Corruption Law in Public Sector (2019), *available at* https://www.lp.gov.lb/backoffice/uploads/files/1-%20قانون%20مكافحة%20الفساد%20و%20انشاء%20الهيئة%20الوطنية%20لمكافحة%20الفساد.pdf.

3 Palestine Anti-Corruption Law (2005), *available at* https://www.aman-palestine.org/reports-and-studies/8645.html.

4 Kenya Anti-Corruption and Economic Crimes Act 2003, Act no. 3 of 2003, The Kenya Gazette, Apr. 11, 2008, 756-70.

5 U4 Anti-Corruption Resource Center, International Good Practice in Anti-corruption Legislation (2010), *available at* https://www.u4.no/publications/international-good-practice-in-anti-corruption-legislation/.

India, covers offences like taking a bribe, criminal misconduct (including amassing of disproportionate assets) by a public servant, and mandates prior government sanction for prosecution. In 2011, India ratified the United Nations 2005 Convention against Corruption (UNCAC) and agreed to bring its domestic laws into line with it. The UNCAC counts giving and taking a bribe, illicit enrichment and possession of disproportionate assets by a public servant as offences, and it addresses bribery of foreign public officials and bribery in the private sector. In August 2013, the Prevention of Corruption (Amendment) Bill 2013 was introduced in the Indian Parliament to amend the 1988 Act. The 'Statement of Objects and Reasons' of the Bill says that it was introduced to bring the 1988 Act into line with the UNCAC.[1]

The American Anti-Corruption Act sets up a framework for city, state and federal laws to fix the broken political system. It fundamentally reshapes the rules of American politics and restores the people as the most important stakeholders in the political system. The act has three primary goals: first, to stop political bribery so that special interests cannot use job offers and donations to influence politicians. Second, ending secret money, so people know who is buying political power. Third, fixing U.S. broken elections so the people, not the political establishment, are the ones in control.[2]

Implicit laws and regulations. In many countries, civil and criminal law provisions regulate corruption-related offences by including a definition of these offences as well as laying down enforcement provisions. They typically consist of a list of practices and behaviors that are made illegal, and provide for adequate sanctions and penalties which should also serve as a deterrent for would-be corrupt

1 The Prevention of Corruption (Amendment) Bill (2013), *available at* https://www.prsindia.org/sites/default/files/bill_files/1376983957~~PCA_Bill_2013_0.pdf.

2 Represent.Us, *supra* note 254.

officials.[1] These practices include bribery, nepotism and conflict of interest or favoritism in the awarding of contracts or provision of government benefits. As criminals find more innovative ways to enrich themselves and circumvent the law, some countries prefer to set out a general standard, broadly criminalizing the "abuse of public office for private gain".

A current example of how corruption is regulated in criminal law is Qatar's penal code no. 11 of 2004, amended by Law No. (2) of 2020, in which forms of corruption such as bribery are regulated and this has been updated, with foreign bribery also criminalized, as in the following:

> *whereby if a foreign employee who works for a public institution or international organization in the State accepts bribery, he shall be punished with a maximum term of ten years and a fine of double the bribery, or if he committed the crime to facilitate the international trade. Moreover, the person who gives a bribe shall be exempted from punishment if he reported to the authorities before the investigations take place.*[2]

In addition, the new amendments stress the penalization of abuse of authority/power by official employees. They expand the scope of the penal code to any crimes committed outside Qatar if such crimes are directed to internal or external security of the state, or if they are crimes related to bribery, embezzlement of public funds, counterfeiting currencies or official documents or stamps, or circulation of any counterfeited currencies. Another new mechanism originating in criminal law in the United Kingdom is the unexplained wealth order (UWO), which can be made in respect of any property valued at more than £50,000, wherever in the world it is situated, if a court

1 U4 Anti-Corruption Resource Center, *supra* note 262.

2 Law no. 2 of 2020, introducing some amendments to the Penal Code no. 11 of 2004 (Qatar).

is satisfied that there is reasonable cause to believe that a person has an interest in it and reasonable grounds to suspect that they would not have been able to obtain that property using their lawfully obtained income from known sources. Once the order has been issued, the person will be given a limited amount of time in which to respond. A failure to respond can be relied upon in civil recovery proceedings under the Proceeds of Crime Act 2002. It reverses the burden of proof to require the person to prove that the property is not the proceeds of crime, rather than requiring the state to prove that it is. Regardless of whether civil recovery proceedings are commenced, the response can be used to inform other investigations, including criminal ones.[1] This mechanism has the potential to curb the number of corrupt practices resulting in monetary gain. In summary, criminal law plays a huge role in fighting numerous forms of corruption, even if the word 'corruption' is not cited directly.

Corruption is regulated in civil law in an indirect manner. Once a criminal offence is acknowledged, civil damages are awarded. So civil law does not regulate corruption, but it provides for contract validity and damages remedies. Civil actions are indicative of the want of better alternatives to recovery.[2] Civil law partly deals with evidential proof and has an impact on the proof of corruption. Proof of evidence is submitted on a general principle of loyalty (fairness), hence it must be obtained and produced in a fair manner. In the context of corruption, the interpretation of this rule has been enlarged.[3] Therefore, in France there are no civil law rules on corruption; yet pursuant to the criminal procedure code, a victim can obtain civil compensation from a criminal law court under

1 Neil Swift et al., *Unexplained Wealth Orders*, Peters & Peters (2017), https://www.petersandpeters.com/expertise/unexplained-wealth-orders/.

2 Simon N.M. Young, *Why Civil Actions Against Corruption?* 16 J. Fin. Crim. 144, 144-159 (2009).

3 Béatrice Jaluzot & Michaela Meiselles, Civil Law Consequences of Corruption and Bribery in FRANCE 225-38 (2009).

certain conditions. Civil law's provision of a remedy depends on the decision arrived at under criminal law. Civil law is required to compensate persons who have suffered damage as a result of corruption.

Money laundering laws are used to reveal the roots of corruption, regardless of its form, since wherever there is an act of grand corruption, the proceeds are invariably laundered to conceal their illicit origin.

In the World Bank module on concepts and practical applications of corruption and money laundering, it is suggested that 'Corruption = Financial Gain + Other Benefits'. Thus, acts of corruption as defined in the UNCAC and conduct aimed at hiding the illegal origin of these gains are intrinsically connected.[1] An example illustrating how money laundering laws help in the fight against corruption is the Qatari Law no. 20 of 2019 on 'Combatting Money Laundering and Terrorism Financing'. This showcases how money laundering laws intertwine with anti-corruption efforts and how the two instruments complement each other. Article 30 of Law no. 20 refers to coordination with specialized anti-corruption bodies locally and internationally: "coordination with the administrative control and transparency authority in implementing the United Nations Convention against Corruption". And chapter 8, 'Transparency of Legal Persons and Legal Arrangements', outlines principles which must be respected in order to avoid corrupt practices.[2]

Money laundering laws are another line of defense to prevent perpetrators of corruption escaping punishment, since most

---

1 World Bank, *Module 1: Corruption and Money Laundering: Concepts and Practical Applications*, http://pubdocs.worldbank.org/en/887011427730119189/AML-Module-1.pdf p.7-9 (last visited Nov. 4, 2019).

2 Law no. 20 of 2019 on Combating Money Laundering and Terrorism Financing (Qatar), *available at* http://www.qfcra.com/en-us/whatwedo/AntiMoneyLaundering/Documents/Ref%201.%20AML%20CFT%20Law-Final%20-%20ENG.pdf.

criminals choose to conceal and launder the proceeds of their corrupt acts and practices. Adding another layer of defense can aid in containing the bigger problem – corruption per se – because money laundering laws deal with the proceeds of corrupt actions.

Other Tools

Among the different legal means deployed to fight corruption, there are other, specific tools which do the same job. These are associations, platforms, networks, initiatives and indexes. Far from being an exhaustive list, these examples are illustrations of different anti-corruption strategies adopted internationally.

The **International Association of Anti-Corruption Authorities (IAACA)** is an independent, non-governmental, non-political, anti-corruption organization, composed of institutions responsible for investigation, prosecution and prevention of corruption around the world. It is the umbrella that embraces ACAs worldwide. Over 140 countries and regions participate in the Association through organizational and individual membership. The IAACA was officially established following a meeting held at the UN offices in Vienna, Austria, in April 2006. A handover to Qatar was made in 2015.[1]

Established in 2011 by UNODC, the **Anti-Corruption Academic Initiative (ACAD)** is a central hub for anti-corruption education worldwide. This collaborative project aims at promoting the teaching of and research into anti-corruption issues by higher level education institutions. It brings together professors globally and regionally, fosters networking and offers free online resources. These include, in a number of languages, academic articles, papers and publications covering an extensive range of anti-corruption themes and issues. ACAD has also developed a three-credit multidisciplinary model university course which focuses on the United Nations Convention

1 International Association of Anti-Corruption Authorities [IAACA], https://www.linkedin.com/company/iaacanet (last visited Dec. 18, 2019).

against Corruption. The course is offered in all official UN languages and can be taught as part of, or as a complement to, a degree in law, business or social sciences.[1] An Arabic version of ACAD was established, which covers Arab countries and performs similar duties.

The **International Anti-Corruption Academy (IACA)** was initiated by the United Nations Office on Drugs and Crime (UNODC), INTERPOL, the European Anti-Fraud Office (OLAF), the Republic of Austria and other stakeholders.[2] It is an international organization and post-secondary educational institution, based in Laxenburg, Austria. IACA presents itself as an international, innovative and globally renowned center of excellence, empowering professionals who substantially contribute to the global fight against corruption, and it has become the leading educational institution in the field. Through education, research and cooperation, its goal is to overcome current shortcomings in knowledge and practice in the field of anti-corruption. The academy offers two Masters degrees, one of which is an International Masters in Anti-Corruption Compliance and Collective Action (IMACC) and is specially designed for anti-corruption compliance and collective action professionals involved with the business sector. IACA has adopted a unique approach, which is international in catering to various corners of the globe and observing regional diversity. It is inter-disciplinary, ensuring that all thematic aspects of corruption, including both academic and practical ones, are taken into account; inter-sectoral, linking practitioners with researchers, the public sector with the private sector, and academics with civil society; integrative, providing knowledge and hands-on tools applicable to different parts of the world; and sustainable, offering lasting solutions.[3]

1 *Education*, UNODC, https://www.unodc.org/unodc/en/corruption/education.html (last visited Dec. 18, 2019).

2 *About Us*, Int'l Anti-Corruption Academy [IACA], https://www.iaca.int/who-we-are/about-us/faq.html (last visited Nov. 2, 2019).

3 *Id.*

The **European Anti-Fraud Office (OLAF)** is the only EU body mandated to detect, investigate and stop fraud using EU funds. This body focuses on developing policy and carrying out independent investigations into fraud and corruption involving EU funds, to restore trust in EU institutions. It has investigative powers in matters relating to fraud, corruption and other offences affecting EU financial interests and expenditure. The main spending categories are structural funds, agricultural policy and rural development funds, direct expenditure and external aid; some areas of EU revenue, mainly customs duties; and investigating suspicions of serious misconduct by EU staff and members of EU institutions. OLAF has proved its effectiveness through its success stories, where a wide range of wrongdoing, from embezzlement, fraudulent claims and misconduct in public procurement procedures, to customs fraud have been investigated.[1] Another effective approach adopted by OLAF is the Hercule Program Fund actions, which aim to prevent and combat fraud, corruption and other illegal activities affecting the EU's financial interests. Actions eligible for funding include technical and operational investigation support and specialized training and research activities, and they are implemented via grants and contracts.

The **European Partners Against Corruption (EPAC)** network was initiated in 2001 under the auspices of the Belgian Presidency of the European Union. It is an independent, informal network bringing together more than seventy anti-corruption authorities and police oversight bodies from Council of Europe member countries. Of diverse origin, they have different kinds of competences and varied legal forms. The European Anti-Fraud Office (OLAF) mentioned above is a member, whereas the authority of Kosovo enjoys observer status.

1 Eur. Comm'n Reg. 883/2013, OLAF Regulation (Sept. 11, 2013), *available at* https://eur-lex.europa.eu/legal-content/EN/TXT/?uri=CELEX%3A02013R0883-20170101.

EPAC offers a medium for practitioners to share experiences, identify opportunities and co-operate across national borders in developing common strategies and high professional standards.

The **Anti-Corruption Strategy for the Legal Profession** project is a global initiative that raises awareness among legal professionals about existing international anti-corruption instruments and equips lawyers with the necessary tools and knowledge to identify, address and resolve potential threats to the integrity of the legal profession caused by corruption. The project came into existence via three influential anti-corruption related bodies: the International Bar Association (IBA), in cooperation with the Organization for Economic Co-operation and Development (OECD) and the UN Office on Drugs and Crime (UNODC). It offers a comprehensive insight into ways of managing the risks of corruption in order to meet the demands and requirements of clients; the role lawyers play in combating international corruption; and how international instruments and extraterritorial legislation apply to legal practice. Major outcomes of this project were the following publications: 'Risks and Threats of Corruption and the Legal Profession',[1] 'Anti-Corruption Compliance and the Legal Profession', 'The Client Perspective'[2] and the 'Anti-Corruption Ethics and Compliance Handbook for Business'.[3]

The UNDP's Global Program on Anti-Corruption for Development Effectiveness (PACDE) came to an end on 31 December 2013[4] and was succeeded by the UNDP's **Global Anti-Corruption**

1 OECD, Risks and Threats of Corruption and the Legal Profession (2010).

2 OECD, Anti-Corruption Compliance and the Legal Profession –The Client Perspective (2013).

3 OECD, Anti-Corruption Ethics and Compliance Handbook for Business (2013).

4 UNDP, UNDP Global Thematic Program on Anti-Corruption for Development Effectiveness (PACDE), https://www.undp.org/content/dam/aplaws/publication/en/publications/democratic-governance/dg-publications-for-website/pacde-global-programme-on-anti-corruption/PACDE_brochure_white.pdf

Initiative (GAIN) in 2014. GAIN has five main objectives: to integrate anti-corruption solutions in service delivery; strengthen state/institutional capacity to implement the UNCAC and prevent corruption; mitigate corruption risks in climate finance and natural resource management; enhance civic engagement, youth and women's empowerment for increased transparency and accountability at national and local levels; and improve results-based management and institutional effectiveness on anti-corruption.

GAIN's strategy is as follows:

- Expanding the political and normative agenda on anti-corruption to development plans, by integrating anti-corruption in service delivery and other sectors (e.g. climate change and extractive industries).
- Strengthening state/institutional capacities (the supply side of anti-corruption) to prevent and combat corruption, working with line ministries and oversight institutions, including parliamentarians.
- Promoting civic engagement and social accountability (the demand side of anti-corruption) through youth and women's empowerment and the participation of civil society and the media.
- Improving results-based management and institutional effectiveness for effective implementation of anti-corruption initiatives and monitoring their results.[1]

The **European Union Anti-Corruption Initiative (EUACI)** is the biggest EU support program in the area of fighting against corruption in the Ukraine. It is co-funded and implemented by the Ministry of Foreign Affairs of Denmark and it consolidates efforts directed at assisting Ukraine's anti-corruption campaign. The

---

(last visited Dec. 4, 2019).

1 UNDP, UNDP Anti-Corruption Initiative (GAIN) 2014-2017 8 (2015), *available at* https://www.undp.org/content/undp/en/home/librarypage/democratic-governance/anti-corruption/undp-global-anti-corruption-initiative--gain--2014-2017.html.

overall objective of the EU and Danish funding is to improve implementation of anti-corruption policy, thereby ultimately contributing to a reduction in corruption. The program aims to strengthen the capacity of newly-created anti-corruption institutions and enhance external oversight over the reform process. It consists of three main components: strengthening the operational and policy-making capacities of state institutions trying to prevent and fight against corruption; strengthening the Parliament's oversight of reform implementation and its capacity to scrutinize and improve the strategic legislative framework; and enhancing the capacity of local bodies, civil society and media to contribute to the fight against corruption.[1]

The **Group of States Against Corruption (GRECO)** embodies the approach of the Council of Europe in the fight against corruption, which has always been multidisciplinary and consists of three interrelated elements: the setting of European norms and standards; monitoring of compliance with the standards; and capacity building offered to individual countries and regions, through technical co-operation programs. The Council of Europe has developed a number of multifaceted legal instruments dealing with matters such as the criminalization of corruption in the public and private sectors, liability and compensation for damage caused by corruption, the conduct of public officials and the financing of political parties. Examples of such instruments are: the Criminal Law Convention on Corruption (CETS 173),[2] the Civil Law Convention on Corruption (CETS 174),[3] Twenty Guiding Principles for the Fight Against Corruption Resolution 97/24,[4] an additional protocol

---

1 Eur. Union Anti-Corruption Initiative, *The Primary Goal of EUACI in Ukraine*, https://euaci.eu/who-we-are/about-programme (last visited Dec. 4, 2019).

2 Criminal Law Convention on Corruption, *supra* note 110.

3 Civil Law Convention on Corruption, *supra* note 214.

4 Council of Europe, Comm. of Ministers Res. 97/24 On the Twenty Guiding Principles against Corruption Resolution (1997).

to the Criminal Law Convention on Corruption (CETS 191),[1] Recommen-dation on Codes of Conduct for Public Officials and Recommendation on Common Rules against Corruption in the Funding of Parties and Electoral Campaigns No. R (2000) 10.[2] These instruments are aimed at improving the capacity of states to fight corruption domestically as well as at the international level. The monitoring of compliance with these standards is entrusted to the Group of States against Corruption (GRECO).[3]

The **Stolen Asset Recovery Initiative (StAR Initiative)** is the outcome of a partnership between the World Bank Group and the United Nations Office on Drugs and Crime (UNODC), which supports international efforts to end safe havens for corrupt funds, as the proceeds of corruption are often laundered in the world's financial centers and these criminal flows are a drain on social services and economic development programs, contributing to the further impoverishment of the world's poorest countries.[4] StAR works with developing countries and financial centers to prevent the laundering of the proceeds of corruption and to facilitate more systematic and timely return of stolen assets. StAR provides platforms for dialogue and collaboration and also facilitates contact among different jurisdictions involved in asset recovery. It has a public database that tracks efforts by prosecution authorities worldwide as they go after assets gained from corruption. The database compiles and systematizes information about completed and

---

1 Additional Protocol to the Criminal Law Convention on Corruption, E.S.T 191 (May 15, 2003).

2 Council of Europe, Comm. of Ministers, Rec. No. R (2000) 10 on Codes of Conduct for Public Officials and Recommendation on Common Rules against Corruption in the Funding of Parties and Electoral Campaigns.

3 *Council of Europe, The Fight against Corruption: A Priority for the Council of Europe*, https://www.coe.int/en/web/greco/about-greco/priority-for-the-coe (last visited Nov. 2, 2019).

4 Jean-Pierre Brun et al., Asset Recovery Handbook: A Guide for Practitioners xi (2011).

ongoing active corruption cases involving international asset recovery.[1]

The international NGO **Global Witness** was founded in 1993 to protect human rights and the environment by fearlessly confronting corruption and challenging the systems that enable it. Global Witness calls for a better world, where corruption is challenged and accountability prevails, all can thrive within the planet's boundaries and governments act in the public interest. Global Witness's pioneering work emphasizes the link between natural resources, conflict and corruption. It investigates and campaigns to prevent resource-related conflict and corruption, and associated environmental and human rights abuses. From investigations to high-level lobbying meetings, it aims to engage on every level where it might make a difference and bring about change. Since the very first campaign to shut down the Khmer Rouge's illegal logging industry, Global Witness has uncovered the truth about blood diamonds and helped bring trillions of oil, gas and mining revenues into the open. A spotlight was directed onto the brutal killings of those defending their land from forced seizure by corporations and governments alike. The organization also campaigned for an end to the use of anonymous companies and much more.[2] Global Witness believes that the only way to protect people's rights to land, livelihoods and a fair share of their national wealth is to demand total transparency in the resources sector, ensure sustainable and equitable resources management, and prevent the international financial system from propping up resource-related corruption.[3]

Global Financial Integrity (GFI) is a think tank based in Washington D.C., producing high-caliber analyses of illicit financial

1 Stolen Asset Recovery Initiative (StAR), *StAR Asset Recovery Watch Database & Settlements Database*, https://star.worldbank.org/corruption-cases/?db=All (last visited Dec. 4, 2019).

2 *About Us*, Global Witness, https://www.globalwitness.org/en/about-us/ (last visited Nov. 2, 2019).

3 Global Witness, Skoll Found., http://skoll.org/organization/global-witness/ (last visited Nov. 2, 2019).

flows, advising the governments of developing countries on effective policy solutions and promoting pragmatic transparency measures in the international financial system as a means to achieving global development and security. GFI has focused on a number of core corruption-related issues, such as money laundering, transitional crimes, illicit financial flows, trade fraud, anonymous companies, tax havens and bank secrecy.[1]

The **World Economic Forum Partnering Against Corruption Initiative (PACI)** shapes the global anti-corruption agenda, supports regional initiatives and facilitates industry projects of collective action. It has taken on the responsibility of publicly showing leadership in the fight against corruption, reinforcing corporate commitment to integrity, values and ethics, and providing a competitive advantage for companies by becoming the preferred choice of ethically concerned customers/consumers. One of the biggest challenges facing the anti-corruption movement is encouraging collective action to rebuild trust in business and institutions. Undeniably, corrupt practices differ across political and industry systems, and accordingly, PACI activities incorporate distinctive international best practices that are solutions-based and forward looking. PACI is the foremost CEO-led anti-corruption initiative. Working alongside international organizations, academics and government institutions, PACI is at the forefront of industry practices to rebuild and foster trust in business and institutions.[2]

In 2013, in Botswana, the **Commonwealth Africa Anti-Corruption Centre (CAACC)** was established with a remit to support member countries in fighting procurement irregularities, bribery, money laundering and other financial crimes. A body bringing together anti-corruption authorities from twelve Common-wealth

1 *About Us*, Global Financial Integrity, https://gfintegrity.org/about/ (last visited Dec. 4, 2019).

2 PACI Vanguard, Partnering Against Corruption Initiative (PACI) (2018), *available at* http://www3.weforum.org/docs/WEF_PACI_Vanguard.pdf.

countries in the African region, CAACC uses its convening power to connect government officials, professionals and practitioners, and provides technical and legal assistance for them to deliver solutions tailored to the needs of member countries.[1] The Center guides public sector institutions, lawmakers, judges and enforcement agencies in Commonwealth member countries in their efforts to strengthen and protect the rule of law, good governance, democracy and human rights. It further assists in developing and implementing anti-corruption strategies in collaboration with civil society and business. CAACC's effectiveness stems from its wide scope, which ranges from drafting legislation to ensuring that new and emerging natural resources industries are protected from abuse, to upholding the integrity of sport by helping countries to stamp out bribery and match fixing.[2]

There are a number of anti-corruption tools which produce measurable results, such as indices, surveys and barometers. These should be able to show what is happening on the ground. Some people criticize such tools, since they are heavily based on opinion, which might not be impartial. Others think they can provide the legislature and reformers with guidance as to changes which need to be made. Below are examples of such tools, which include the Corruption Perception Index (CPI), Global Corruption Barometer (GCB) and Control of Corruption Governance Metric (CC).

The **Corruption Perception Index (CPI)** is a composite indicator which aggregates data from a number of different sources. These sources provide the perceptions of country experts and

1 Andrew Maramwidze et al., *By Fighting Illicit Financial Activity, the Commonwealth Africa Anti-Corruption Centre Aims to Promote Growth and Stimulate Investment in Its Members' Economies*, AACA (Jun. 1, 2018), https://www.accaglobal.com/my/en/member/member/accounting-business/2018/06/insights/commonwealth-africa.html.

2 *The Commonwealth Tackling Corruption*, The Commonwealth, https://thecommonwealth.org/tacklingcorruption (last visited Dec. 4, 2019).

businesspeople of the level of corruption in the public sector.[1] CPI has been defined as a list of the countries of the world which shows how much corruption is thought to exist among its public officials and politicians, and it is published by Transparency International.[2] CPI is based on thirteen sources which collect the assessment of experts and business executives on specific forms of corrupt behavior in the public sector (i.e. bribery, diversion of public funds, use of public office for private gain, nepotism in the civil service and state capture).[3] The higher the score, the better the outcome. The measuring scale of CPI runs on a 0-100 scale, where 0 equals the highest level of perceived corruption and 100 equals the lowest level of perceived corruption.[4] This index publishes its results annually.

Whereas the CPI is almost exclusively focused on perceptions by elites (business people and experts), the **Global Corruption Barometer (GCB)** provides information on perceptions of corruption by the general public.[5] Also created by TI, it surveys a wider audience, directly interacting with people and asking them to share their experience and how far countries have to go to fight corruption. It is considered to be the world's largest survey which asks citizens about their direct personal experience of corruption in their daily lives.[6] Sample questions include citizens being asked whether

---

1 Corruption Perception Index, Honk Kong Ind. Comm'n Against Corruption (2019), https://www.icac.org.hk/en/intl-persp/survey/corruption-perceptions-index/index.html.

2 *Corruption Perception Index*, Cambridge Dictionary, https://dictionary.cambridge.org/dictionary/english/corruption-perceptions-index, (last visited Dec. 4, 2019).

3 Marcos Álvarez-Díaz et al., Corruption Perceptions Index 2017 Statistical Assessment 9 (2018).

4 *Id.*

5 Alexander Hamilton & Craig Hammer, *Can We Measure the Power of the Grabbing Hand? A Comparative Analysis of Different Indicators of Corruption* 20 (World Bank Econ. Dev. Data Group, Policy Research Working Paper 8299, 2018).

6 *Global Corruption Barometer: Citizens' Voices from Around the World*, Transparency Int'l (2017), https://www.transparency.org/news/feature/global_corruption_barometer_citizens_voices_from_around_the_world [hereinafter *Global Corruption Index*].

they had paid a bribe for public services which they may have received. Respondents were asked whether "corruption had a not significant/somewhat significant/very significant effect on (1) personal and family life, (2) the business environment, and (3) political life".[1] In Europe and Central Asia, they were asked whether their household had paid a bribe for any of eight public services.[2]

The **Control of Corruption Governance Metric (CC)** is one of the six World Governance Indicators (WGI).[3] It captures perceptions of the extent to which public power is exercised for private gain, including both petty and grand forms of corruption, as well as "capture" of the state by elites and private interests. As with the CPI, 0 is the lowest and 100 the highest rank.

Reference has already been made in general terms to an important anti-corruption tool, which will now be discussed in detail. This is the United Nations Convention Against Corruption (UNCAC).

---

1 Hamilton & Hammer, *supra* note 301, at 21.

2 *Global Corruption Index*, *supra* note 302.

3 The Worldwide Governance Indicators (WGI) are a longstanding research project to develop cross country indicators of governance. The WGI consist of six composite indicators of broad dimensions of governance covering over 200 countries since 1996: voice and accountability, political stability and absence of violence/terrorism, government effectiveness, regulatory quality, rule of law and control of corruption. These indicators are based on several hundred variables obtained from 31 different data sources, capturing governance perceptions as reported by survey respondents, non-governmental organizations, commercial business information providers and public sector organizations worldwide. *See* Daniel Kaufmann et al., The Worldwide Governance Indicators: Methodology and Analytical Issues 2 (2010).

CHAPTER THREE:
THE UNITED NATIONS CONVENTION AGAINST CORRUPTION (UNCAC)

I am therefore very happy that we now have a new instrument to address this scourge at the global level.

– Kofi A. Annan, Secretary-General of the United Nations from 1997 – 2006, in his introduction to the UNCAC[1]

UNCAC is the only international legally binding instrument which addresses corruption. It is the mother or guardian of all anti-corruption laws.

In the UNCAC introduction, the UN secretary-general at the time, Kofi Annan, stated that:

> *Corruption undermines democracy and the rule of law, leads to violations of human rights, distorts markets, erodes the quality of life and allows organized crime, terrorism and other threats to human security to flourish. This evil phenomenon is found in all countries—big and small, rich and poor—but it is in the developing world that its effects are most destructive. Corruption hurts the poor disproportionately by diverting funds intended for development, undermining a government's ability to provide basic services, feeding inequality and*

1 UNCAC iv.

injustice and discouraging foreign aid and investment. Corruption is a key element in economic underperformance and a major obstacle to poverty alleviation and development.[1]

This shows why issuing a comprehensive instrument such as UNCAC was important. Moreover, one of the main aims of having a standalone binding instrument was to create a sense of responsibility for all involved parties and competent bodies, regardless of their legal status – since NGOs and civil society are also involved – for collaborating and cooperating in restraining corrupt conduct in the most effective way possible.

UNCAC caters to different stakeholders, such as the U.N. itself, national governments, independent bodies, the public and private sectors, NGOs, civil society and citizens, so it involves everyone. It is also worth noting that the UN Office on Drugs and Crime (UNODC) serves as secretariat for UNCAC, specifically the Corruption and Economic Crime Branch (CEB) in the Division for Treaty Affairs (DTA).

It acts as an international legal instrument which forms a reference point against which laws can be drafted. As was stated by the ad hoc committee for UNCAC at the time:

The Convention offers all countries a comprehensive set of standards, measures and rules that they can apply to strengthen their legal and regulatory regimes to prevent and control corruption.[2]

UNCAC is an overarching anti-corruption instrument which asserts the cross-border nature of corruption and offers both preventive and punitive measures. It also adopts a flexible attitude in

1 UNCAC iii.

2 Dimitri Vlassis, UNODC, The United Nations Convention against Corruption. Overview of Its Contents and Future Action, Resource Material Series No. 66, at 118.

phrasing its provisions; some measures carry an obligation to adopt them[1] and others contain strongly recommended or optional provisions[2] (see the UNCAC appendix).

It is important to realise that although UNCAC is a legally binding instrument, it is classified as a convention and not as a law. And, surprisingly, although it is the only international instrument explicitly assigned to fight corruption, it does not define corruption itself. Instead, it defines acts of corruption, including bribery, embezzlement, money laundering, concealment and obstruction of justice.

Going back to the Convention's components, it consists of seventy-one articles in eight chapters, with substantive provisions illuminating a range of important subjects. The eight chapters will now be examined in detail: chapter 1 on "General Provisions"; chapter 2 on "Preventive Measures"; chapter 3 on "Criminalization and Law Enforcement"; chapter 4 on "International Cooperation"; chapter 5 on "Asset Recovery"; chapter 6 on "Technical Assistance and Information Exchange"; chapter 7 on "Mechanisms for Implementation"; and chapter 8 on "Final Provisions".

3.1 CHAPTER 1 OF UNCAC

The first chapter of UNCAC (Articles 1-4) covers general provisions, use of terms, scope of application and protection of sovereignty. The first article, "General Provisions", summarizes the purpose of issuing the Convention in three main points:

> *(a) to promote and strengthen measures to prevent and combat corruption more efficiently and effectively;*

---

1 Where this phrasing "States Parties shall..." means mandatory. UNCAC arts. 3, 4, 5(1)-(4).

2 Where this phrasing "shall consider adopting…" means Optional. *Id.* arts. 7(2)(3), 8(4)(6), 14(2)(3).

(b) *to promote, facilitate and support international cooperation and technical assistance in the prevention of and fight against corruption, including in asset recovery;*

(c) *to promote integrity, accountability and proper management of public affairs and public property.*[1]

As noted in the text of this article, the Convention covers all relevant levels to combat corruption, starting from the measures already in place, strengthening them and ensuring their effectiveness, to promoting international cooperation. This last element prevents corrupt proceedings from crossing borders and escaping their origins. International cooperation makes a huge difference in regulating such incidences, facilitating asset recovery and restoring such assets to their rightful owners. Therefore, UNCAC emphasizes it, realizing its vital importance.

It is essential to promote the culture of values, as UNCAC does in mentioning integrity and accountability. A simple definition of integrity shows its precious worth. It has been defined as the quality of being honest and having strong moral principles that you refuse to change,[2] so it is a quality of high value that is hard to change. Imagine if all were bound by supreme universal traits such as integrity in all aspects of life and all duties were performed with integrity, what would be the outcome? And how about accountability? An obvious synonym for accountability is responsibility. Yet it is much deeper than it seems in an anti-corruption context. Being self-responsible is using self-discipline to refine oneself until one is the best version possible in all encounters. If this was accomplished, then the rest would surely pan out organically. If individuals hold a true sense of integrity and are accountable, then proper management in the public sector will take its natural course.

---

1 *Id.* art. 1.

2 *Integrity*, Cambridge Dictionary, https://dictionary.cambridge.org/dictionary/english/integrity (last visited Dec. 4, 2019).

In its second article, UNCAC opted to define crucial terms to be understood in light of the Convention, such as public officials. These are:

> *(i) any person holding a legislative, executive, administrative or judicial office of a State Party, whether appointed or elected, whether permanent or temporary, whether paid or unpaid, irrespective of that person's seniority; (ii) any other person who performs a public function, including for a public agency or public enterprise, or provides a public service, as defined in the domestic law of the State Party and as applied in the pertinent area of law of that State Party; (iii) any other person defined as a "public official" in the domestic law of a State Party. However, for the purpose of some specific measures contained in chapter II of this Convention, "public official" may mean any person who performs a public function or provides a public service as defined in the domestic law of the State Party and as applied in the pertinent area of law of that State Party.*[1]

Foreign public officials are:

> *any person holding a legislative, executive, administrative or judicial office of a foreign country, whether appointed or elected; and any person exercising a public function for a foreign country, including for a public agency or public enterprise.*[2]

An official of a public organization is:

> *an international civil servant or any person who is authorized by such an organization to act on behalf of that organization.*[3]

---

1 UNCAC art. 2(a).

2 *Id.* art. 2(b).

3 *Id.* art. 2(c).

Property assets are:

assets of every kind, whether corporeal or incorporeal, movable or immovable, tangible or intangible, and legal documents or instruments evidencing title to or interest in such assets.[1]

Proceeds of crime are:

any property derived from or obtained, directly or indirectly, through the commission of an offence.[2]

Freezing or seizure is:

temporarily prohibiting the transfer, conversion, disposition or movement of property or temporarily assuming custody or control of property on the basis of an order issued by a court or other competent authority.[3]

Confiscations:

includes forfeiture where applicable, shall mean the permanent deprivation of property by order of a court or other competent authority.[4]

Predicate offences are:

any offence as a result of which proceeds have been generated that may become the subject of an offence as defined in article 23 of this Convention.[5]

Controlled delivery is:

the technique of allowing illicit or suspect consignments to pass out of, through or into the territory of one or more States, with

---

1 *Id.* art. 2(d).

2 *Id.* art. 2(d).

3 *Id.* art. 2(f).

4 *Id.* art. 2(g).

5 *Id.* art. 2(h).

the knowledge and under the supervision of their competent authorities, with a view to the investigation of an offence and the identification of persons involved in the commission of the offence.[1]

UNCAC defines essential terms, such as public official, foreign public official, official public organization, property, freezing or seizure, confiscation, predicate offences and controlled delivery in order to ensure an accurate understanding of UNCAC provisions.

UNCAC pays a great deal of attention to the procedural aspect of instances of corruption. This is indicated in the first chapter, particularly article 3, which defines the scope of the UNCAC application to encompass all procedural layovers, including prevention, investigation, prosecution of corruption, freezing, seizure, confiscation and return of the proceeds of offences.

In the last section of the first chapter, in article 4, UNCAC emphasizes the idea of respecting state parties' sovereignty and refraining from intervention in the domestic affairs of other states. This allows justice to take its natural course in each country, in alignment with the existing regulatory environment, and creates more room for innovative ways to incorporate UNCAC's provisions. There is no room for artificial transplants of foreign legal practices which do not fit local realities on the ground.

3.2 CHAPTER 2 OF UNCAC

To return to the notion of ex ante mentioned previously, what should be done before corruption happens? How can it be prevented? Articles 5-14 of the second chapter of UNCAC contain a set of preventive measures, covering all stages and sectors and a number of critical areas, namely: public, private, judiciary, public prosecution,

1 *Id.* art. 2(i).

civil society and individuals, public procurement and money laundering. In addition, there are special preventive policies and procedures and assigned authorities to monitor the whole procedure. Below is a description of each sector and area.

In the public sector, along with the values of integrity, honesty and responsibility, UNCAC focuses on human capital holistically, starting from recruitment, selection criteria, hiring, retention, training, rotation, adequate remuneration, promotion, equitable pay scales, disciplinary measures, retirement and, most importantly, the reporting mechanisms to appropriate authorities about acts of corruption. The public servant should receive proper training to enhance their awareness of the risks of corruption. This also applies to those in elected public office and political parties. Among other strategies, in order to double the effect of UNCAC's measures in the public sector, state parties to the Convention are required to issue codes of conduct for public officials: "the correct, honorable and proper performance of public functions", as stated in article 8 (2).[1]

One would expect that UNCAC would pay special attention to the judiciary and prosecution sectors, since they are influential, yet vulnerable to corruption. A code of conduct for members of the judiciary was necessary and the same applied to the prosecution services.[2]

In the private sector, UNCAC recommends auditing mechanisms to enhance ethics, integrity and transparency in the private sector. It further calls for civil, administrative or criminal penalties for failure to comply with such measures. This is all pursuant to article 12 in the Convention. It also tackles the notion of conflict of interest, where:

> *former public officials join the private sector after retirement or resignation where such activities or employment relate directly*

1 *Id.*

2 *Id.* art. 11.

to the functions held or supervised by those public officials during their tenure.[1]

From a structural viewpoint, UNCAC addresses the establishment of businesses and private sector organizations, calling for clear and transparent legal identity and appropriate regulating procedures, such as subsidies and licenses granted by public authorities for commercial activities. It further underlines the importance of books and records, financial statement disclosures and accounting and auditing standards, in order to prevent off-book records or transactions. It closes the article with a reference to manipulation that occurs in the area of taxes, where disguised bribery can occur. For example, "deductibility expenses that constitute bribes",[2] pursuant to articles 15 and 16.

Sometimes systematic approaches do not have the same impact that society does. In this case, a question must be asked: what is the purpose of issuing a law or designing a policy? The simple answers to this are: to regulate certain forms of behavior, to give and protect certain rights. However, what if the people practicing corruption have an active role in activating, contributing to or participating in law and decision making? This is dealt with in article 13 of UNCAC, which defines "the people" clearly as "groups outside the public sector, such as civil society, non-governmental organizations and community-based organizations".[3] It further elaborates on this and calls for active participation from such people, whether in preventing or fighting corruption, or increasing public awareness of it. Public access to information is granted and participation encouraged in corruption-related educational programs. The subject has therefore become part of school and university curricula. Access is guaranteed to relevant anti-corruption

1 *Id.* art. 12(e).

2 *Id.* art. 12(4).

3 *Id.* art. 13(1).

bodies mentioned earlier in the Convention. Of course, limitations to such liberties are set to avoid loose ends and uncontrolled activities. Article 13 (1) has this proviso: "if the freedom granted does not respect rights or reputations or threatens national security or public order, public health or morals".[1]

Cultivating a culture of transparency was a key driver of UNCAC ambitions. This is stated in article 10, which promotes access to information about the work of public administration, such as its organization, functioning and decision-making processes, with periodic reports on the risks of corruption to be publicly available. The article further urges that simplifications be made to administrative procedures, to facilitate public access to the competent decision-making authorities, as stated in section (b) of article 10.[2]

In terms of prevention, the main focus of chapter 2, UNCAC targets specific areas of concern, such as public finance, procurement and money laundering. In systems of public procurement and management of public finance, UNCAC states that both shall be founded upon a basis of transparency, competition and objective criteria in decision-making. This approach is further explained in the text of article 9.[3] In the sphere of public finance, it is stated that national budget procedures should be adopted. In the public procurement field, procurement procedures and participation conditions should be announced and distributed in advance and in a clear manner. As for money laundering and its historical ties to corruption mentioned several times in previous sections of this book, before stating what UNCAC has to say about money laundering, it should first be defined.

> *Money laundering is the processing of these criminal proceeds to disguise their illegal origin. This process is of critical*

1 *Id.*

2 *Id.* art. 10(b).

3 *Id.* art. 9.

importance, as it enables the criminal to enjoy these profits without jeopardizing their source.[1]

UNCAC allocates a separate preventive measure to money laundering, following its method in other chapters, dedicating a whole chapter to this phenomenon. This is enough to justify and prove the existence of money laundering in the corruption hemisphere. Thus, in article 14, the importance of instituting a comprehensive anti-money laundering regulatory and supervisory regime is indicated. This regime should be able to detect and monitor the movement of cash and appropriate negotiable instruments across borders. Article 14[2] also addresses all concerned actors, including banks and non-bank financial institutions. It asks financial institutions and money remitters to scrutinize transfers of funds more carefully and to retain such information throughout the payment chain.

Chapter 2 ensures that effective preventive policies and procedures are set in place in accordance with UNCAC's provisions, whilst adding that a thorough assessment of the current regulatory environment of the concerned country should be conducted, with a view to determining its adequacy to prevent and fight corruption. In addition, collaboration with international and regional organizations is encouraged, to promote and develop the measures, all pursuant to article 5.[3] UNCAC follows on from this logically in article 6,[4] which states the necessity of having a body or bodies to fulfil the responsibilities set out in article 5, focusing on anti-corruption knowledge sharing and awareness.

---

1 *What Is Money Laundering*, FATF, https://www.fatf-gafi.org/faq/moneylaundering/ (last visited Nov. 2, 2019).

2 UNCAC art. 14.

3 *Id.* art. 5.

4 *Id.* art. 6.

3.3 CHAPTER 3 OF UNCAC

The third chapter of UNCAC turns from mere directive provisions to the arena of implementation: criminalization and law enforcement. In articles 15-42, UNCAC begins by listing corruption related offenses, then proposes law enforcement mechanisms and penalties, and finally provides for further protection, since retaliation is inevitable in some corruption cases. Before scrolling down the list, certain terms should be defined.

Term number one, bribery, is:

> *an attempt to make someone do something for you by giving the person money, presents, or something else that they want.*[1]

Term number two, embezzlement, is:

> *The offense of stealing...the public money.*[2]

Term number three, trade influence, is:

> *the situation where a person misuses his/her influence over the decision-making process for a third party (person, institution or government) in return for his loyalty, money or any other material or immaterial undue advantage.*[3]

Term number four, abuse of functions, is described as follows:

> *abuse of functions occurs when an employee or office holder uses their position to perform an illegal act, or an act that he/she has no legal authority to do, to pursue a private gain. It usually*

---

1 *Bribery*, Cambridge Dictionary, https://dictionary.cambridge.org/dictionary/english/bribery (last visited Oct. 10, 2019).

2 *What is Embezzlement*, The Law Dictionary, https://thelawdictionary.org/peculatus/ (last visited Oct. 10, 2019).

3 Christian, *Trading in Influence*, AALEP (Apr. 2, 2015), http://www.aalep.eu/trading-influence.

results in either a benefit or damage to others. The failure to act can also constitute an abuse of functions.[1]

Term number five is illicit enrichment. According to the UNCAC definition, it is:

a significant increase in the assets of a public official that he or she cannot reasonably explain in relation to his or her lawful income.[2]

Term number six is the proceeds of crime. The UNCAC definition says that this is:

any property derived from or obtained, directly or indirectly, through the commission of an offence.[3]

Term number seven, concealment, is:

the improper suppression or disguising of a fact, circumstance, or qualification which rests within the knowledge of one only of the parties to a contract, but which ought in fairness and good faith to be communicated to the other, whereby the party so concealing draws the other into an engagement which he would not make but for his ignorance of the fact concealed.[4]

Term number eight, obstruction of justice, is:

The noncompliance with the legal system by interfering with (1) the law administration or procedures, (2) not fully disclosing information or falsifying statements, and (3) inflicting damage on an officer, juror or witness.[5]

---

1 *Abuse of Function*, GAIN Integrity, https://www.ganintegrity.com/portal/corruption-dictionary/ (last visited Nov. 4, 2019).

2 UNCAC art. 20.

3 *Id.* art. 2(e).

4 Black's Law Dictionary (9th ed. 2009).

5 *Id.* (defining obstruction of justice).

As mentioned above, chapter 3 initially lists corruption-related offences which state parties should consider incriminating, namely: 1. Bribery of national public officials,[1] 2. Bribery of foreign public officials and officials of public international organizations,[2] 3. Embezzlement, misappropriation or other diversion of property by a public official,[3] 4. Trading in influence,[4] 5. Abuse of functions,[5] 6. Illicit enrichment,[6] 7. Bribery in the private sector,[7] 8. Embezzlement of property in the private sector,[8] 9. Laundering of proceeds of crime,[9] 10. Concealment,[10] 11. Obstruction of justice.[11]

Chapter 3 then proposes law enforcement mechanisms and penalties, emphasizing the "liability of legal persons and it called for the broadest liability possible as the liability of legal persons may be criminal, civil or administrative",[12] pursuant to article 26. The Convention further restricts whoever tries to engage in any sort of corrupt practices by carefully defining all the relevant legal terminology, leaving no room for claiming immunity. Thus, the following terms are regulated: participation and attempt,[13] knowledge, intent and purpose as elements of an offence,[14] the statute of limitations,[15] prosecution, adjudication and sanctions,[16] and jurisdiction.[17] Chapter 3 also highlights

---

1 UNCAC art. 15.
2 *Id.* art. 16.
3 *Id.* art. 17.
4 *Id.* art. 18.
5 *Id.* art. 19.
6 *Id.* art. 20.
7 *Id.* art. 21.
8 *Id.* art. 22.
9 *Id.* art. 23.
10 *Id.* art. 24.
11 *Id.* art. 25.
12 *Id.* art. 26.
13 *Id.* art. 27.
14 *Id.* art. 28.
15 *Id.* art. 29.
16 *Id.* art. 30.
17 *Id.* art. 42.

further penalties, such as freezing, seizure and confiscation.[1]

As stated earlier, many corruption cases are associated with retaliation. Therefore, article 32 regulates for protection of witnesses, experts and victims,[2] and article 33 for protection of reporting persons, also known as whistleblowers.[3] The provided protection includes physical protection and relocation, in order to guard against unjustified treatment and potential retaliation or intimidation. Besides these provisions, the Convention grants the victim "a right to initiate legal proceedings against those responsible for that damage in order to obtain compensation".[4]

To ensure that all the above-mentioned measures are efficiently enforced, the Convention asserts the necessity of having an established, independent, specialized authority[5] with law enforcement powers. In order to reduce corruption-related offenses, it also highlights the importance of multi-sectorial cooperation between law enforcement authorities[6] and national authorities,[7] and national authorities and the private sector.[8] Both bank secrecy provisions and criminal records should serve as means of helping to obtain convictions for corruption-related offences. Thus it advocates for: "appropriate mechanisms available within its domestic legal system to overcome obstacles that may arise out of the application of bank secrecy laws".[9] The Convention indicates that previous convictions of an alleged offender, regardless of their location, should be made available to be used in criminal proceedings dealing with "an offence established in accordance with this Convention".[10]

---

1 *Id.* art. 31.
2 *Id.* art. 32.
3 *Id.* art. 33.
4 *Id.* art. 35.
5 *Id.* art. 36.
6 *Id.* art. 37.
7 *Id.* art. 38.
8 *Id.* art. 39.
9 *Id.* art. 40.
10 *Id.* art. 41.

3.4 CHAPTER 4 OF UNCAC

Since the beginning of this book, there have been countless instances where corruption and its proceeds have been described as mutant, transnational and cross border in nature. A connection has therefore been made between corruption and money laundering, and global organizations fighting corruption have always kept this notion in mind when creating any new instrument or issuing corrective policies. Indeed, right at the beginning, before even UNCAC existed, this link between corruption and transnational/cross border activities was acknowledged in the official statements of UNTOC and many other UN bodies. Therefore, allocating a whole chapter in UNCAC to international cooperation was necessary to avoid falling short when it came to enforcement. International cooperation in criminal matters comes in many forms: extradition, transfer of sentenced persons, mutual legal assistance, transfer of criminal proceedings, law enforcement cooperation, joint investigations and special investigative techniques.

If a public servant or an employee in the public sector embezzles some money and moves it outside the country into a foreign bank account or buys real estate in another country, how can these stolen assets be recovered? What can be done when corruption-related proceeds leave their origin? How does the corrupt individual him/herself deal with this? How can UNCAC help in addressing the problem? Articles 43-50 of chapter 4 handle a variety of issues. Article 43 is an invitation to state parties to "consider assisting each other in investigations of and proceedings in civil and administrative matters relating to corruption".[1] The first part of the article refers to civil and administrative matters, while the second is devoted to criminal matters. It is clear that corruption is not a trivial thing and its drastic consequences deserve the toughest penalty possible; so in

1 *Id.* art. 43.

section 2 of article 43, UNAC emphasizes the matter of dual criminality, which means: "that an act or omission must be considered criminal in two states, one of which is the state where the crime is prosecuted".[1] This in its turn affects extradition, which is applicable when the act in question forms a criminal offence under the laws of both state parties. In this particular case, dual criminality is fulfilled, whether offences belong to the same category at both ends or even if they are denominated.[2]

Article 44 deals with extradition. Extradition is: "the act of making someone return for trial to another country or state where they have been accused of doing something illegal".[3] UNCAC comprehensively regulates extradition, attempting to include all possible cases, to prevent evasion, even if many 'ifs' appear. These include instances where several offences have been committed and only one is related to the article, or if the offence is considered to involve a fiscal matter. If there is no extradition treaty, UNCAC can still be considered as "the legal basis for extradition in respect of any offence to which this article applies".[4]

Further to the above, UNCAC allows:

> *the transfer to their territory of persons sentenced to imprisonment or other forms of deprivation of liberty for offences established in accordance with this Convention in order that they may complete their sentences there.*[5]

---

1 Van den Wyngaert, *Double Criminality as a Requirement to Jurisdiction*, in Double Criminality, Studies in International Criminal Law 43-56 (Nils Jareborg ed., 1989).

2 UNCAC art. 43.

3 Extradition, Cambridge Dictionary, https://dictionary.cambridge.org/dictionary/english/extradition (last visited Dec. 4, 2019).

4 UNCAC art. 44(5).

5 *Id.* art. 45.

UNCAC further encourages state parties to accomplish this via bilateral or multilateral agreements. And if several jurisdictions are involved, then a transfer of criminal proceedings is allowed by the provisions of UNCAC in article 47, to fulfill "the interests of the proper administration of justice, with a view to concentrating the prosecution".[1]

UNCAC adopts an exhaustive approach in mutual assistance. It emphasizes that it should be conducted in the broadest manner possible, further asserting that such assistance should be offered to the fullest extent in investigations, prosecutions and judicial proceedings, and it elaborates on forms it may take, such as "(a) Taking evidence or statements from persons; (b) Effecting service of judicial documents; (c) Executing searches and seizures, and freezing assets".[2] UNCAC also details the structural aspect of this mechanism, including a statement of what a mutual assistance request should contain:

> *(a) The identity of the authority making the request; b) The subject matter and nature of the investigation, prosecution or judicial proceeding to which the request relates and the name and functions of the authority conducting the investigation, prosecution or judicial proceeding; (c) A summary of the relevant facts, except in relation to requests for the purpose of service of judicial documents; (d) A description of the assistance sought and details of any particular procedure that the requesting State Party wishes to be followed;*[3]

It also lists grounds for postponing and refusal of mutual assistance, and examples of this include: 1. "it interferes with an ongoing investigation, prosecution or judicial proceeding".[4] 2. "if execution

1 *Id.* art. 47.

2 *Id.* art. 46(3)(a)-(c).

3 *Id.* art. 46(15)(a)-(d).

4 *Id.* art. 46(25).

of the request is likely to prejudice its sovereignty, security, public order or other essential interests".[1]

From a law enforcement perspective, these provisions could either take UNCAC to a different level or leave it as toothless paperwork, ineffective in the real world. Therefore, it is important to highlight the provisions among elements of international cooperation. Law enforcement is: "the activity of making certain that the laws of an area are obeyed".[2] This is accomplished using various means, such as effective information sharing, exchange of personnel and other experts, direct cooperation between law enforcement agencies, and also joint investigations and special investigations with controlled delivery,[3] both on a case-by-case basis, ensuring that the sovereignty of the state party where the investigation is conducted is fully respected.[4] UNCAC states the importance of protecting sovereignty in its general provisions in chapter 1(4).

3.5 CHAPTER 5 OF UNCAC

Chapter 5 provides another answer to the question of how to retrieve assets stolen and moved into a foreign bank account within the country of origin or across international borders. In articles 51-59 of chapter 5, UNCAC regulates asset recovery before it happens, by means of prevention, and after it happens. It also names the concerned bodies in

1 *Id.* art. 46(21)(b).

2 *Law Enforcement*, Cambridge Dictionary, https://dictionary.cambridge.org/dictionary/english/law-enforcement (last visited Dec. 4, 2019).

3 Controlled delivery: shall mean the technique of allowing illicit or suspect consignments to pass out of, through or into the territory of one or more States, with the knowledge and under the supervision of their competent authorities, with a view to the investigation of an offence and the identification of persons involved in the commission of the offence. UNCAC art. 2(i).

4 *Id.* art. 49.

this procedure. The definition of property, according to article 2 of UNCAC, is: "assets of every kind, whether corporeal or incorporeal, movable or immovable, tangible or intangible, and legal documents or instruments evidencing title to or interest in such assets".[1]

The preventive section of UNCAC emphasizes the necessity of enhanced scrutiny and disclosure systems according to the domestic law of the concerned state party, stipulating that financial institutions are required "to verify the identity of customers, to take reasonable steps to determine the identity of beneficial owners of funds deposited into high-value accounts"[2] and further, when individuals are, or have been, entrusted with prominent public functions, there should be increased scrutiny. This extends to the families of the concerned individuals and their close associates. In article 52,[3] UNCAC advocates for robust financial disclosure systems that require public officials to disclose their assets and financial accounts, regardless of their location. In case of non-compliance, sanctions should be applied. These measures demonstrate that justice is blind to status and is applied to whoever breaches the law.

Another measure taken by UNCAC in chapter 5 to prevent money laundering is regulation against shell banks. FATF, the key organization driving anti-money laundering efforts around the world, defines shell banks as the following:

> *Shell bank means a bank that has no physical presence in the country in which it is incorporated and licensed, and which is unaffiliated with a regulated financial group that is subject to effective consolidated supervision. Physical presence means meaningful mind and management located within a country. The existence simply of a local agent or low-level staff does not constitute physical presence.*[4]

1 *Id.* art. 2(d) (defining property).

2 *Id.* art. 51(1).

3 *Id.* arts. 52(5)-(6).

4 Financial Action Task Force, International Standards on Combating Money

UNCAC does not miss the significance of such phenomena and the Convention therefore demands that state parties, particularly their regulatory and oversight bodies, should ban the establishment of shell banks and refrain from dealing with them.

After the damage has been inflicted, the question to ask is: what solutions are offered by UNCAC? The answer lies in the text of article 53 and its measures for direct recovery of property. These grant the harmed party the following: 1. Right to initiate a civil case,[1] 2. Compensation or damages;[2] where the former is awarded due to a criminal act or non-contractual situation and the latter is usually used in a civil litigation context for tortious acts or contractual breach. 3. Confiscation.[3] As per UNCAC provisions, "Confiscation, which includes forfeiture where applicable, shall mean the permanent deprivation of property by order of a court or other competent authority".[4]

Even if the solutions offered by UNCAC as stated above exist, it is more important to know how they are implemented, especially if the assets have left their origin. What are the mechanisms to restore them to their rightful owners? An answer is provided in article 54, which examines mechanisms for recovery of property through confiscation, based upon international cooperation.[5] Provided that there is a reasonable basis for the confiscation, authorities are

---

Laundering and the Financing of Terrorism & Proliferation – The FATF Recommendations 124 (2019).

1 "(a)*to initiate civil action in its courts to establish title to or ownership of property acquired through the commission of an offence established in accordance with this Convention*". UNCAC art. 53(a).

2 "(b)*to pay compensation or damages to another State Party that has been harmed by such offences*". *Id.* art. 53(b).

3 *"(c) Take such measures as may be necessary to permit its courts or competent authorities, when having to decide on confiscation, to recognize another State Party's claim as a legitimate owner of property acquired through the commission of an offence established in accordance with this Convention"*. *Id.* art. 53(c).

4 *Id.* art. 2(g) (defining confiscation).

5 *Id.* art. 54.

permitted to temporarily prohibit the transfer, conversion, disposition or movement of property, or they can temporarily assume custody or control of property on the basis of a confiscation order issued by a court or other competent authority.[1] Additional measures may preserve the property for confiscation on the basis of a foreign arrest or criminal charge associated with the purchase of such property.[2]

Is this enough to fully implement asset recovery solutions? It is crystal clear that international cooperation is vital for effective asset recovery, as referenced before in chapter 4. International cooperation is crucial simply to get things going. Article 55 regulates all the details of international cooperation procedures facilitating confiscation. An example of one such detail is the act of sharing relevant information for execution, including:

> *description of the property to be confiscated, including, to the extent possible, the location and, where relevant, the estimated value of the property and a statement of the facts relied upon by the requesting State Party sufficient to enable the requested State Party to seek the order under its domestic law.*[3]

It also provides for grounds for cooperation refusal, e.g. lack of sufficient and timely evidence, or if the property is of a *de minimis* value.[4] According to article 56, conditional special cooperation is also permitted in circumstances of disclosing information on proceeds of offences that:

> *might assist the receiving State Party in initiating or carrying out investigations, prosecutions or judicial proceedings or might*

1 *Id.* art. 2(f) (defining "freezing" or "seizure").

2 *Id.* art. 45.

3 *Id.* art. 55(3)(b).

4 *Id.* art. 55(7).

lead to a request by that State Party under this chapter of the Convention.[1]

A final important question to ask is: what happens after property is confiscated? Where does it end up? The simple answer is: "return to its prior legitimate owners". Yet, the answer to this question is tackled in detail in the provisions of article 57, which regulate the return and disposal of assets.[2]

Adding an extra layer of enforcement serves to guarantee and further legitimize all listed means and efforts. UNCAC requires state parties to: first (as stated in chapter 4, article 59)[3] ensure effective international cooperation via bilateral or multilateral agreements; and second, to establish a financial intelligence unit (FIU) responsible for receiving, analyzing and disseminating to the competent authorities reports of suspicious financial transactions.[4]

3.6 CHAPTER 6 OF UNCAC

An important question needs to be asked here: how is it possible to ensure that whoever is responsible for applying all that UNCAC has to offer is capable and qualified? This is specifically addressed by UNCAC to avoid wasting the desired outcomes of this global instrument. The Convention includes certain provisions (in articles 60-62) to ensure fulfilment of the maximum potential of such states or individuals. Among these measures, UNCAC requires state parties to develop specific training programs for its personnel who are responsible for preventing and combating corruption.[5] It also emphasizes

1 *Id.* art. 56.
2 *Id.* art. 57.
3 *Id.* art. 59.
4 *Id.* art. 58.
5 *Id.* art. 60(1).

the technical assistance aspect, especially for the benefit of developing countries, in their plans and programs.[1] It highlights the need for back up for operational and training activities in international and regional organizations according to relevant agreements or arrangements,[2] and it further encourages state parties to adopt voluntary approaches to financial contribution to UNODC and to developing and transition countries, for the sake of the best implementation of UNCAC in such regions.

UNCAC dedicates an entire provision to fine tuning international cooperation from the information management angle, in article 61. This article is concerned with collection, exchange and analysis of information on corruption. Its provisions define how information should be analyzed, taking into consideration trends within the concerned territory, and further vetting it through circumstances in which corruption offences are committed.[3] The article further focuses on information concerning corruption, such as statistics, and urges the sharing of analytical expertise among international and regional organizations. This is to aid in developing common definitions, standards and methodologies, as well as gathering information on best practices to prevent and combat corruption.[4]

Due to the size of corruption as a problem and its negative effect on society in general, and in particular on sustainable development, UNCAC lays down other measures to secure fruitful implementation of the Convention, emphasizing economic development and technical assistance. In this context, it can be seen that on the one hand there are state parties and developed countries, while on the other, there are developing countries and economies in transition. UNCAC encourages state parties to cooperate on various levels, to enhance financial, material and technical assistance offered to

1 *Id.* art. 60(2).

2 *Id.* art. 60(3).

3 *Id.* art. 61(1).

4 *Id.* art. 61(2).

developing countries and economies in transition, with a view to strengthening their capacities to prevent and combat corruption.[1]

3.7 CHAPTER 7 OF UNCAC

Moving on from the discussion of chapter 6 and re-phrasing the same logical question asked there one more time, how can UNCAC be assessed in entirety? What is the assurance that it is implemented? Chapter 6 addresses concerned individual and state parties, whilst chapter 7 addresses the Convention itself. If chapter 6 lays down terms ensuring implementation of UNCAC provisions in state parties, who will ensure that the whole process is orchestrated and harmonized? In articles 63 and 64 of chapter 7, this is tackled through two mechanisms. Firstly, the Conference of the States Parties to the Convention[2] (CoSP) is the main policy-making body of the United Nations Convention against Corruption. It supports state parties and signatories in their implementation of the Convention and gives policy guidance to UNODC to develop and implement anti-corruption activities. The Conference meets every two years and adopts resolutions and decisions in furtherance of its mandate. It was created to promote the implementation review mechanisms developed by the UNODC in its capacity as the secretariat to the UNCAC.[3] The second mechanism is the secretariat, which plays an active role in providing the necessary services to the Conference of the States Parties to the Convention. The specific secretariat designations are mentioned in article 64 as the following: "1. Acting as Secretariat to the Conference of the States Parties, 2. Supporting

1 *Id.* art. 62.

2 *Conference of the States Parties to the United Nations Convention against Corruption*, UNODC, https://www.unodc.org/unodc/en/corruption/COSP/conference-of-the-states-parties.html (last visited Dec. 20, 2019).

3 UNCAC art. 63.

the Implementation Review Mechanism, 3. Delivering Technical Assistance and Developing Tools".[1]

3.8 CHAPTER 8 OF UNCAC

UNCAC's final provisions 65-71 invite state parties to adopt all the necessary legislative and administrative measures, in accordance with fundamental principles of domestic laws, to ensure the implementation of the obligations deriving from the Convention. Further, they encourage state parties to resolve disputes which might arise, firstly through negation, then arbitration, and finally the International Court of Justice, according to the terms of article 66.[2] There are various ways in which state parties may reach a UNCAC dispute settlement, and states can opt out of these procedures, and also withdraw their reservations at any time, as long as the Secretary-General of the United Nations is notified of such withdrawal.[3]

Other topics covered in chapter 8 include provisions on signature, ratification, acceptance, approval and accession,[4] and entry into force. The provision covering entry into force is very exact. This occurs on the ninth day after the date of deposit of the thirtieth instrument of ratification, acceptance, approval or accession.[5] Amendments are bound by the expiry of five years from the entry into force of the Convention.[6] Denunciation must be made in writing and the Secretary-General of the United Nations should be notified, as the denunciation will be effective one year after the date of receipt of the notification by the Secretary-General.[7] The depositary is the

1 *Id.* art. 64.

2 *Id.* art. 66.

3 *Id.* art. 66(3)-(4).

4 *Id.* art. 67.

5 *Id.* art. 68.

6 *Id.* art. 69.

7 *Id.* art. 70.

Secretary-General of the United Nations,[1] and the Convention is available in the six official UN languages, which are Arabic, Chinese, English, French, Russian and Spanish.[2]

1. اتفاقية الأمم المتحدة لمكافحة الفساد

2. 联合国反腐败公约

3. United Nations Convention against Corruption

4. CONVENTION DES NATIONS UNIES CONTRE LA CORRUPTION

5. ÊÎÍÂÅÍÖÈß ÎÐÃÀÍÈÇÀÖÈÈ ÎÁÚÅÄÈÍÅÍÍÛÕ ÍÀÖÈÉ ÏÐÎÒÈÂ ÊÎÐÐÓÏÖÈÈ

6. CONVENCIÓN DE LAS NACIONES UNIDAS CONTRA LA CORRUPTION

1 *Id.* art. 71(1).

2 *Id.* art. 71(2).

CHAPTER FOUR:
CORRUPTION IN EDUCATION

The remaining sections of this book will give illustrations of corruption found in everyday life. The decision to focus on three particular sectors connected to people's daily experience was made, firstly, due to personal preference of the author. Secondly, they were selected because most human beings are either exposed to or use elements from these sectors in their daily lives. Thirdly, they are extremely important for many reasons. Corruption in these fields exhausts countries' budgets, which should play a pivotal role in maintaining human progression and development towards a better world. Finally, other sectors such as business and sport deserve a publication all of their own, since their corruption issues involve a plethora of details which should be tackled meticulously.

Whether it is education, health or human rights, three actors are crucial to each sector: provider/performer/recipient.

Everyone has the right to education.
- Article 26, UDHR

Although this sector should logically imply the upholding of honorable and righteous standards, yet in reality it is riddled with many corrupt practices. Education is the basis of everything; it is a universal right.[1] It is a major driver of human and economic development[2] and is the first interaction of most human beings. Education generates knowledge and cultivates systems which many other sectors rely upon. It shapes humanity. Not only does education facilitate people's general knowledge about the world around them, but it also allows them to create an identity for themselves and for their nation.[3]

An education system is a collection of "institutions, actions and processes that affect the 'educational status' of citizens in the short and long run".[4] If the institutions, actions and processes are fairly constituted and performed, then education will have a positive, formative influence on the individual.

Roots of education are bitter, but the fruit is sweet.
– Aristotle

But what if the fruit is also bitter? What if there are glitches in the system? Will it corrupt those who are being educated? Education is built upon a number of key actors and components, namely: education providers (schools, universities, education performers, administrative staff, teachers and academics); and education recipients (end users, who are students, the designated audience). In this chapter, two cases per actor or component will be presented, building on this basic hypothesis: if the education system is clean (corruption free), then human outcomes are too. If it is not, then many undesirable consequences will follow and greater problems will result.

1 G.A. Res. 217 (III) A, Universal Declaration of Human Rights art. 26 (Dec. 10, 1948).

2 *Education*, Transparency Int'l, https://www.transparency.org/topic/detail/education (last visited Dec. 20, 2019).

3 Eric Uslaner & Bo Rothstein, All for One: Equality, Corruption, and Social Trust 228 (2006).

4 Mark Moore, *Creating Efficient, Effective, and Just Educational Systems through Multi-Sector Strategies of Reform* (Oxford Univ. RISE Working Paper 15/004, 2015).

Education without values, as useful as it is, seems rather to make man a more clever devil.
– C. S. Lewis

> *From corruption in the procurement of school resources and nepotism in the hiring of teachers, to the buying and selling of academic titles and the skewing of research results, major corruption risks can be identified at every level of the education and research systems.*[1]

This is how the Global Corruption Report describes corruption in education. This report is a helpful reference that catalogues numerous interesting real-life cases of corruption in education sectors around the world. It will be employed in this chapter to highlight cases linked to each actor and component of the education system.

4.1 EDUCATION PROVIDERS

The corrupt behavior of education providers such as schools and universities manifests in various forms, including admission bribes, research fund embezzlement, resources stolen from education budgets, books and supplies sold instead of being given out freely, [2] seat trading. It is worth focusing here on two of these: unjust admission and fund manipulation.

4.1.1 Unjust Admission

Corruption has been defined in previous chapters as private over public interest. This occurs at different stages of the admission process and sometimes based on different motives. Some students

1 Transparency Int'l, *supra* note 170.

2 *Education*, *supra* note 419.

might be accepted in return for a bribe or as a result of nepotism and elite social status. Others might be rejected based on their ethnicity, color or gender. Quite simply, admission can be bought without any regard to qualifications, in order to obtain financial or other benefits. Many education providers have lost their reputation and trust due to such unjustified, arbitrary and suspicious decisions.

This form of corruption happens in the foyer of institutions offering what is supposed to be a universal right granted to everyone. In Nigeria, for example, one million students pass college entrance exams, yet there are only 300,000 places available in public universities. Limited access to education has no doubt contributed to the use of bribes and personal connections to gain coveted places at universities, with some admissions officials reportedly working with agents to obtain bribes from students. Those who have no ability or willingness to resort to corruption face lost opportunities and unemployment.[1].

It is worth noting that in the United States at one time a financial incentive system existed which allowed recruiters to be given compensation incentives on the basis of the number of students enrolled, until a congressional ban of 1992 barred all schools from such financial incentives.[2] It is sadly common nowadays that most educational institutions are driven by money rather than quality education, which in its turn undermines the quality of admitted students and consequently the quality of graduates. The number of probes into the qualifications of fake degree holders are on the rise and admission scandals are reported as well. The common denominator is money, whether it is graduates using money to buy a degree, or would-be students paying to get into an educational institution. From a legal perspective, these acts are forbidden by criminal law.[3] Looking at it from an abstract

1 *Nigerian Universities Demand Bribes for Admission*, Global Post (May 11, 2012); Transparency Int'l, *supra* note 170.

2 *Id.* at 163.

3 To use academic degrees without authorization, under the German Criminal Code § 132a.

point of view, payment is made for something illegal to be given in return. Of course, if education is approached through normal legitimate channels, then anyone wishing to get a degree has to do the necessary (study, pass the exam). Corrupt institutions have a nickname. They are called degree/diploma mills and are defined as: "an organization that gives educational qualifications to people in exchange for money, without them having to do any or much studying".[1]

Whoever wants to be admitted to these diploma mills needs only to pass the minimum admission requirements. Nowadays there are a number of institutions whose whole existence is dependent on granting degrees in return for money. To prove this, one only has to enter the sentence "buy a degree" into any search engine online. Before the sentence has been fully typed, the engine will start suggesting options for completing it and a surprising number of results will appear.

4.1.2 Fund Manipulation

Since unjust admission happens in the foyer of the education provider, the question now is what happens inside the system of that provider? An educational system is often judged by its outcomes — how students perform, how high research standards are, how materially well-equipped institutions are, and how ready to carry out their duties. If everything mentioned meets the common standard, then one can initially evaluate the system and form an idea about its efficiency. But what if it falls beneath the standard? What if the outcomes do not reflect the budget allocated for quality education? The answer lies with fund manipulation. If this has penetrated the fabric of the educational system, it may result in a degradation in the education level of generations, not to mention other subsidiary implications which cause people to engage in other activities to secure their basic need for education.

1 *Diploma Mills*, Cambridge Dictionary, https://dictionary.cambridge.org/dictionary/english/diploma-mill (last visited Dec. 4, 2019).

4.1.3 Research Fund Embezzlement

OLAF and Guardia di Finanza unravel complex scam with EU funds for nautical devices.
The European Anti-Fraud Office (OLAF) put an end to an intricate fraud scheme through which more than 1.4 million euro-worth of European Union funds, meant for emergency response hovercraft prototypes, had been misappropriated. Operation Paper Castle stretched over several EU Member States, and relied on OLAF's close cooperation with Guardia di Finanza, in Italy. OLAF uncovered the complicated fraud scheme as part of its investigation into alleged irregularities in a Research and Innovation project granted to a European consortium. The Italian-led consortium, with partners in France, Romania and the United Kingdom (UK), was tasked with creating two hovercraft prototypes to be used as emergency nautical vehicles able to reach remote areas in case of environmental accidents. During on-the-spot checks performed in Italy by OLAF and Guardia di Finanza, OLAF investigators discovered various disassembled components of one hovercraft, as well as another hovercraft which was completed after the deadline of the project. It became evident that, in order to obtain the EU funds, the Italian partners falsely attested to the existence of the required structural and economic conditions to carry out the project. Investigative activities carried out by OLAF in the UK revealed that the British partner only existed on paper. The company was in fact created and owned by the same Italian partners. To simulate the actual development of the project and to divert funds, fictitious costs had also been recorded. In practice, once the EU funds were obtained, the Italian grantees used accounting artifices to syphon off money, forging documents denoting false expenses. A thorough analysis of more than 12 000 financial transactions and payments made in the project showed that part of

the EU funds received by the Italian and UK partners had been used to extinguish a mortgage on a castle facing foreclosure - today subject to seizure. OLAF ascertained that the castle officially belonged to a different British company, originally established by the same Italian couple, but now owned by a US company, from Delaware. Further enquiries uncovered that the Italian couple also created and owned the above mentioned US company. OLAF concluded its investigation in November 2017 with two judicial recommendations – to the Public Prosecutor's Office of Genoa and to the City of London Police in the UK – and a financial recommendation to the Directorate-General for Research and Innovation of the European Commission. Guardia di Finanza is investigating the persons concerned for embezzlement and fraud against the EU, false accounting, fraudulent bankruptcy and fraudulent statements. Operation Paper Castle is a testament to the pertinent results of the close and constant cooperation between OLAF, Guardia di Finanza and the police forces of Member States. The transnational nature of the investigation meant OLAF played a decisive role, from stem to stern, being able to map out and put an end to the complex fraudulent activity which stretched across several Member States".

– Embezzlement of Research Funding – PRESS RELEASE No 01/2018, 16 February 2018, from OLAF[1]

4.2 EDUCATION PERFORMER

The corrupt behavior of education performers such as administrative staff and academics manifests in various forms, including

1 Eur. Anti-Fraud Office, *OLAF and Guardia Di Finanza Unravel Complex Scam with EU Funds for Nautical Devices* (Feb. 16, 2018), https://ec.europa.eu/anti-fraud/media-corner/news/16-02-2018/olaf-and-guardia-di-finanza-unravel-complex-scam-eu-funds-nautical_en.

practicing with false or forged degrees, academic dishonesty, and teachers and lecturers being appointed through family connections and without qualifications. Grades can be bought as well. Some teachers force students to pay for tuition outside of class.[1] Among these forms of corruption, forged degrees and degree mills, unfair appointments and plagiarism will be discussed in detail here.

4.2.1 Forged Degrees

Germany is one of the only countries which displays doctoral qualifications on passports and identity cards.[2] Many interesting cases have been cited in the Global TI Corruption Report about fake degrees, as shown below:

> *In 2010 a German politician and a member of the German Parliament, had to pay a 5,000 (US$6,159) fine because he had misused his title, claiming a doctoral degree in economics that was not officially recognized in Germany.*[3] *He received this doctoral degree from the 'Freie Universität Teufen', a former institution in Switzerland that allegedly sold academic degrees.*[4]
>
> *A former professor of the Institute of the History of Medicine at the University of Würzburg is suspected of having*

1 *Education*, *supra* note 419.

2 Transparency Int'l, *supra* note 170, at 179 (citing *Nicht ohne meinen Doktortitel*, Süddeutsche.de (Germany) (Jul. 14, 2011).

3 *CDU-Politiker muss Geldstrafe zahlen*, Stern.de (Germany) (May 7, 2010. Jasper had to pay only the above mentioned moderate fine because he made a full confession and showed regret. He refused to resign as a Member of Parliament, however, although he had used his void doctoral degree in the electoral campaign. *See id.* referencing Doktortitel ist falsch, das Diplom nicht, Emsdettenervolkszeitung.de (Germany) (Nov. 3, 2010).

4 *Id.* (The 'Freie Universität Teufen' terminated its business at the end of 2009).

supervised and supported dozens of inadequate doctoral theses prior to his retirement in 2005. According to reports, the theses numbered only 35 or so pages and contained sparse meaningful research achievements by the respective doctoral students.[1] *The emeritus professor is suspected of writing parts of the theses and is believed to have accepted donations by doctoral students for his non-profit societies.*[2] *He had already paid a moderate fine because he had accepted 6,000 (US$7,390) from a consultant who connected him with physicians seeking doctoral degrees.*[3] *Two experts from other universities argued that several of the doctoral theses in question did not meet scientific minimum standards, and the University of Würzburg tried to deprive the respective graduates of their degrees.*[4] *The university recently adopted new doctoral regulations for its faculty of medicine.*[5]

4.2.2. Unfair Appointments

The normal course of job application is that one applies for a vacancy that is publicly announced, with all its requirements set out reasonably and clearly. Nowadays, the process is more advanced. There are special job finding platforms and various professional channels exist to provide easy access for job seekers. Yet, certain concerns are always communicated from fresh graduates and other

---

1 *Id.* (referencing Alfred Forchel and Matthias Frosch, interview by Olaf Przybilla, Süddeutsche Zeitung, Germany, 'Die Doktorfabrik', 28/29 May 2011).

2 *Id.* (referencing Süddeutsche Zeitung, Germany, 'Die Angst vor dem Déjà-vu', 31 March 2011).

3 *Id.*

4 *Id.* (referencing Frankfurter Allgemeine Zeitung (Germany), 'Ramschware Dr. med.', 26 October 2011; Mainpost.de (Germany), 'Doktortitel-Affäre: Uni Würzburg will Titel aberkennen', 13 October 2011).

5 *Id.* (referencing Promotionsordnung für die Medizinische Fakultät der Julius-Maximilians-Universität Würzburg vom 10. Juni 2011).

qualified people who wish to fill these publicly posted vacancies. Why are they not called or why is there no response from potential employers? Why do things not go by the book? Who ends up filling these job vacancies? Why do jobs end up being taken by those who shouldn't have them? The simple answer is: nepotism, or the pressure of social status. Nepotism is derived from the Latin word "nepos", which means nephew or grandchildren.[1] It means "favoritism granted to relatives regardless of merit". Further, one dictionary definition explicitly links it to jobs, as in the following: "favoritism shown to relatives or close friends by those in power (as by giving them jobs)".[2]

Because of their family ties. These family ties are the plausible and salient explanation for hiring decisions taken independent of applicants' qualifications for the position. Qualifications may be assumed to have been irrelevant in the hiring process.[3] However, research consistently shows that teacher quality is one of the most important variables for student success.[4]

Forms of favoritism and nepotism are all considered to be corruption, according to Transparency International and also common sense. In its anti-corruption glossary, TI defines nepotism as follows:

> *Form of favoritism based on acquaintances and familiar relationships whereby someone in an official position exploits his or her power and authority to provide a job or favor to a family*

---

1 *Nepotism*, Wordsmith, https://wordsmith.org/words/nepotism.html (last visited Dec. 21, 2019).

2 Xuhua Chen, An English dictionary with AB Index and Frequency 413 (2010) (defining nepotism).

3 A. Darioly & R.E. Riggio, *Nepotism in Hiring Leaders: Is there Stigmatization of Relatives?* 73 Swiss J. Psych., no. 4, 2014, at 243.

4 Frank Adamson & Linda Darling-Hammond, Addressing the Inequitable Distribution of Teachers: What It Will Take to Get Qualified, Effective Teachers in All Communities (2011).

member or friend, even though he or she may not be qualified or deserving.[1]

An example from the Turkish educational system is found in most other countries:

> *Teachers state that favoritism is experienced to a considerable extent in the provincial education directorate as well as in the Ministry of National Education. Teachers indicate that the practice of favoritism takes place in … the appointment of teachers to schools … It is also significant that favoritism is experienced in selecting teachers to join in-service seminars and courses although all teachers have the right to take part in these seminars and courses.*[2]

Such actions are a prime example of corruption, since making such appointments deprives deserving, qualified individuals of opportunity. Such individuals are to be treasured and capitalized on, as they have devoted their lives to in-depth study of their specific field of science; ultimately to pay it forward to future generations. This is how educators should be perceived and valued. Education is driven by curiosity and eagerness for knowledge. If he/she who is educating others does not possess knowledge, what will the outcome be? Understanding and avoiding such risks should prevail over the temptations of money, power and other benefits.

Yet when corruption knocks at the door of any action, decision or sector and begins its silent work, it starts multiplying rapidly. It might start off with unfair appointments and extend to the post appointment stage, meaning it touches on promotion as well. A trail

1 *Nepotism*, Transparency Int'l, https://www.transparency.org/glossary/term/nepotism (last visited Dec. 21, 2019).

2 Ismail Aydogan, *Favoritism in the Turkish Educational System: Nepotism, Cronyism and Patronage*, 4 Educ. Pol'y Analysis & Strategic Res., no. 1, 2009, at 14.

of negative implications leads from such actions. When an unqualified person gets the job, now that he/she has been injected into the system and the basis of that injection was void, then further void implications will thrive, like promoting this person, or granting remunerations and other benefits. This will have negative consequences and create frustration in the work atmosphere, but the effect will be even greater and not only confined to the toxic work environment. These actions cultivate a new paradigm for younger generations, making them think that things ought to work this way. "Short cut humans" are created as a result. Here is an example from the field of higher education in Italy:

> *Heads of Italian university departments, known as baroni or barons, were awarding qualifications based on exchanges of favors, or to serve private or professional interests, rather than on merit. As of 2017, a total of 59 people were under investigation, seven were placed under house arrest for corruption, and 22 were banned from holding academic posts for 12 months.*[1]

Taking immediate action is necessary to maintain a healthy proportion of hard workers vs lazy ones. There are numerous policy reforms and newly passed laws which have attempted to combat corrupt practices, yet when individuals merely say no to such actions, this can flip the game and make a huge difference.

4.2.3 Plagiarism

This form of corruption involves education providers and education recipients. Both have reasons to commit plagiarism, which has

1 Monica Kirya, Corruption in Universities: Paths to Integrity in the Higher Education Subsector 11 (2019), *available at* https://www.u4.no/publications/corruption-in-universities-paths-to-integrity-in-the-higher-education-subsector (citing C. Edwards).

many root causes. The publication of scientific articles is linked to dividends for an academic career, which is a motivation for teachers to resort to plagiarism. From a researcher or student perspective, it is even easier to see why it happens. Many people perceive plagiarism to be an academic crime which leads to deterioration in one's creativity. The link between corruption and plagiarism has been acknowledged by many scholars and organizations.[1] Here are some comments on the subject:

> *Buying academic papers. "Gifted authorship" has been perceived as the most obvious form of plagiarism, in great part due to the fact that "essay factories" are available online at any moment. The grey market of academic works is present online without any cover-up, in the form of tens of websites that boast of their professionalism and tradition.*

Numerous manifestations of such actions have been documented across the world. For instance:

> *The Austrian Agency for Research Integrity reported about several recent cases, including double submission of the same proposal or authorship conflict. The latter case was a conflict between a PhD student and her supervisor, which made it impossible for her to defend her dissertation in Austria ('Research Integrity Practices in Science Europe Member Organizations' 2016 Survey Report).*[2]

To sum up, the act of plagiarism is considered to be a form of corruption. It is extremely important for academics and others always

---

1 Organizational Immunity to Corruption: Building Theoretical and Research Foundations 126 (Agata Stachowicz Stanusch ed., 2010).

2 Elena Denisova-Schmidt, European Higher Education Area: The Impact of Past and Future Policies 65 (2018).

to be aware of the risks when creating any sort of content. They should be original and refrain from taking what is not theirs without giving proper acknowledgement for the work taken from others.

4.3 EDUCATION RECIPIENTS

The corrupt behavior of education recipients, such as students, manifests in various forms. Two of these will be discussed in detail here: cheating and buying grades.[1]

4.3.1 Cheating and Buying Grades

To cheat is to "behave in a dishonest way in order to get what you want".[2] Cheating is a form of corruption practiced by those who have a mentality of "anything to get ahead". This has unfortunately been normalized and woven into various cultures around the world. Cheating has been recognized and despised in all its aspects throughout human history; and here the focus is on the type of cheating that occurs when people get to the finish line without running the whole route, using the short cut instead. This is how cheating happens. It is considered corruption, since it constitutes a breach of trust. Breaching trust over and over again will inevitably train and grow the muscle of corruption. Unfortunately, "those who cheat their way through school bring with them a culture of cheating everywhere".[3]

Before the digital evolution, cheating was committed through means such as cheat sheets, or "ponies": "a traditional 'pony' is a very

1 *Corruption by topic – Education*, Transparency Int'l, https://www.transparency.org/topic/detail/education (last visited Dec. 27, 2019).

2 *Cheat*, Cambridge Dictionary, https://dictionary.cambridge.org/dictionary/english/cheat (last visited Dec. 27, 2019).

3 Mesharch W. Katusiime, *Exam Cheating a Form of Corruption*, PML Daily (Oct. 17, 2019), https://www.pmldaily.com/oped/2019/10/mesharch-w-katusiimeh-exam-cheating-a-form-of-corruption.html.

small handwritten or typed sheet of paper that can be hidden in the palm of the hand or under clothes".[1]

Nowadays, people have developed innovative ways of cheating; for instance, by using phones, recorders, web links, etc.

Buying grades can occur in various ways. A teacher may ask students for money in return for a grade raise. Others accept gifts. Whether it is the former or the latter, both are illegal and incriminating. They are a form of bribery which in its turn constitutes a form of corruption. To be clearer, bribery is:

> *offering, promising, giving, accepting or soliciting of an advantage as an inducement for an action which is illegal, unethical or a breach of trust. Inducements can take the form of money, gifts, loans, fees, rewards or other advantages (taxes, services, donations, favors etc.).*[2]

How can this be prevented in real life scenarios? One must understand that grades are not priced; in principle, a student is not obliged or required to pay in return for his grade. A student should expend time and effort in preparing and studying for exams. Money, gifts and favors should not be involved at all. If they are, then a red flag should be waved to stop such acts from happening.

The following case is an example of how cheating and buying grades both constitute acts of corruption:

> *On Tuesday, March 12, the U.S. Attorney for the District of Massachusetts announced his office had filed criminal charges*

---

1 Elena Denisova-Schmidt, Academic Dishonesty or Corrupt Values: The Case of Russia 10 (2015), *available at* https://anticorrp.eu/wp-content/uploads/2015/03/Russia.pdf.

2 *What is Bribery*, Transparency Int'l, https://www.antibriberyguidance.org/guidance/5-what-bribery/guidance (last visited Dec. 28, 2019).

against fifty people in a massive college admissions scandal. In the first scheme, parents allegedly paid Singer to help their children cheat on the ACT and SAT college admissions exams. Singer would have the parents change their child's test location to one of two testing centers where Singer had relationships with test administrators who would accept bribes to facilitate the cheating. Singer would then usually arrange for Mark Riddell, a counselor at a private school in Florida, to travel to the test center, purportedly to "proctor" the students taking the exam. Riddell would either coach the students on the proper answers or change their answers after they were done in order to obtain the test score desired by the parents. Parents typically paid Singer between $15,000 and $75,000 for each such exam, and Singer typically paid Riddell $10,000 per student. The second scheme involved Singer bribing college coaches to designate students as recruited athletes (thus facilitating their admission) even though the students in question were not qualified. This scheme frequently involved parents and associates of Singer creating phony application materials and profiles that falsely portrayed the students as star high school athletes. Parents made payments either to Singer's foundation or, in some cases, directly to athletic programs at the universities. Singer would then either pay the coaches directly or make payments to university athletic departments or private sports clubs controlled by the coaches in exchange for the coach's agreement to sponsor the student for admission.[1]

As noted from the above case, cheating can be induced and grades can be bought. Condoning cheating as normal will backfire as a paradigm generator:

---

1 Randall Eliason, *When Is Cheating a Crime? The College Admissions Case*, Sidebars (Apr. 2, 2019), https://sidebarsblog.com/cheating-crime-college-admissions-case/.

To condone cheating is to breed pretenders — the sort that would cheat with the end in view of acing the grades needed for an excellent academic record, which would pave the way for hotshot jobs after graduation. To condone cheating is to breed crooks — the sort that would in the future see no harm in, say, skimming off the top of a public works contract or in making a pile at Customs.[1]

1 *From Cheating Come Crooks, Pretenders*, Philippine Daily Inquirer (Sept. 26, 2019), https://opinion.inquirer.net/124208/from-cheating-come-crooks-pretenders.

CHAPTER FIVE:
CORRUPTION IN HEALTHCARE

Healthy citizens are the greatest asset any country can have.
– Winston Churchill

As implied by Churchill, healthy human beings are needed to make the other sectors run smoothly.

The importance of the health sector has been globally recognized. It is referred to in the U.N.'s Millennium Development Goals (MDGs). There are "*eight goals—three of which (numbers 4, 5 and 6) are health-specific*".[1] The United Nations' Sustainable Development Goal (SDG) number 3 is:

> *good health and well-being: ensure healthy lives and promote well-being for all at all ages; by focusing on providing more efficient funding of health systems, improved sanitation and hygiene, increased access to physicians and more tips on ways to reduce ambient pollution, significant progress can be made in helping to save the lives of millions.*[2]

A well-functioning health sector is a major game changer. Its impact is not only easily evaluated, but it can be tangibly felt by

1 Goal 4: reduce child mortality, Goal 5: improve maternal health, Goal 6: combat HIV\AIDS, malaria and other diseases. Jillian Clare Kohler, UNDP, Fighting Corruption in the Health Sector. Methods, Tools and Good Practices 11 (2011).

2 UNDP, *Goal 3: Good Health and Well-being*, UN.org, https://www.un.org/sustainabledevelopment/health/ (last visited Dec. 30, 2019).

people. As long as the health system is performing under regular circumstances and no complaints are being voiced, then all is well. This is usually the case in almost all 'relaxed economy' countries; meaning, where everyone can access health care services of a reasonable standard. Yet what about countries with unstable, pressured economies, which are far from being relaxed? What happens once the system is tested? Tests and trials are sometimes the results of human actions or circumstances beyond human control. Such actions or events cause turbulence and expose weaknesses in the system, which become noticeable. Corrupt management is a serious problem, and examples of this within the health care system include manipulating budgets allocated to health care, unjustified preferential insurance services, diverted resources and low quality medical staff. The byproduct of such actions is normally failure of healthcare systems:

> *World Bank surveys show that in some countries, up to 80 per cent of non-salary health funds never reach local facilities. Ministers and hospital administrators can siphon millions of dollars from health budgets. Or they can accept bribes. This distorts policy and denies people hospitals, medicines and qualified staff.*[1]

In contrast, events beyond human control are not planned or expected. Take the current pandemic as an example and its violent effects in almost all sectors: education, economy and even politics. It shows the huge impact that a robust health sector has on other sectors and the undesirable, exacerbating effects of an ailing health service. When corruption contaminates the health sector, lives are at stake. And it is not about how poor or rich a country is. Corruption exists and happens in both cases. Countries will suffer according to

---

1 *Corruption by Topic – Health*, Transparency Int'l, https://www.transparency.org/topic/detail/health (last visited Dec. 30, 2019).

how clean or contaminated their health care system is. In some cases, regardless of the economic status of the country, diverted resources can have a far more dreadful impact than any other forces.

It is a regrettable fact that most people globally are not receiving proper health care. There is variation in who is affected by corruption in the health sector. Several quantitative and qualitative studies have shown that poor women are affected the most:[1]

> *a recent study by Amnesty International on maternal health... found that one of the primary causes of the deaths of thousands of pregnant women annually (including during childbirth) is due to corruption by health professionals.*[2]

How can we use the valuable asset mentioned by Churchill in the quote at the beginning of this section?

As in the above pages on the education sector, the focus in this section will be on three factors or "players": healthcare providers (hospitals, health insurance entities, pharmaceutical companies, government ministries); healthcare performers (physicians, nurses, lab technicians); and healthcare recipients or end users (patients).

5.1 HEALTHCARE PROVIDERS

Hospitals will be taken as a convenient example. Numerous corrupt practices of healthcare providers include diverting resources for private gain and exploiting people as subjects of clinical trials for financial gain.

---

1 Kohler, *supra* note 455, at 6.

2 *Id.*

5.1.1 Diverting Resources for Private Gain

> *The WHO world health organization estimates that global health care expenditure is about US$4.7 trillion, this translates into about US$260 billion lost globally to fraud and error. Fraud in the health care system includes the pocketing of user fees by a service provider or the overcharging of a health insurance agency by a physician. In a hospital, it could involve the diversion of patient fees or collusion between a hospital administrator and a purchasing agent.*[1]

This is the horrible truth that lies beneath diverted resources. Whether it is fraud or embezzlement, both roads lead to Rome. "Rome" here is an ironic reference to the destination of such actions. These roads both lead to a sick healthcare system infected with the disease of corruption. When a government allocates a certain amount of money for the health sector – this is called the health budget – it delegates to a designated institution the job of channeling the funds into serving the ultimate goal of having a "well-established healthcare system". Money is given and released from government responsibility under this assumption, and yet one witnesses a repeated scenario of failure to provide good healthcare. Was there not enough money to do so? Or what was the problem exactly? Where did the money go? What do health providers do with it? If it is not utilized, where is it? When individuals who are willing to take advantage of the system are factored in, things become entangled.[2] A real-life scenario from the special care baby unit in Yarmouk Hospital, Baghdad, Iraq, in 2005 illustrates this:

1 *Id.* at 24-25.

2 William D. Savedoff & Karen Hussmann, Transparency Int'l., The Causes of Corruption in the Health Sector: A Focus on Healthcare System 8 (2006).

Despite spending hundreds of millions of dollars on the health ministry, endemic corruption has led to a lack of drugs and helped keep infant mortality and malnourishment rates as high as during the Saddam Hussein era.[1]

And there is evident corruption in Cambodia:

which is reliant on hundreds of millions of dollars per year in overseas development assistance to prop up its health care system, and where known cases of tuberculosis are increasing.[2]

5.1.2 Exploiting People as Subjects of Clinical Trials for Financial Gain

Both healthcare providers and performers may be involved in this practice. It usually occurs during pharmaceutical drug testing or in the course of medical treatment of patients with rare diseases. The targets of such trials are mostly poor, illiterate and desperate sick folks, who will take serious risks to get better:

many multinational companies took advantage of India's favorable regulatory systems by enrolling a large number of illiterate and poor subjects without obtaining adequate informed consent and hence, many unethical trials took place.[3]

It is important to highlight that:

The pharmaceutical sector accounts for a significant portion of

1 *Id.* at 3.

2 *Id.* at 3-4.

3 Kalindi Naik, Clinical Trials in India: History, Current Regulations, and Future Considerations iii (2017).

health budgets globally. Almost a fifth of the entire healthcare budget across OECD countries is spent on medicines.[1]

Further, there is a black market where less fortunate and vulnerable patients are recruited. Those who are in need are willing to volunteer for such trials in return for financial reimbursement. Little do they know that there is no way back once such trials have commenced; therefore, their consent is mischievously obtained. Such patients are defined as:

> *Individuals whose willingness to volunteer in a clinical trial may be unduly influenced by the expectation, whether justified or not, of benefits associated with participation, or of a retaliatory response from senior members of a hierarchy in case of refusal to participate. Examples include patients with incurable diseases, persons in nursing homes, unemployed or impoverished persons, patients in emergency situations, ethnic minority groups, homeless persons, nomads, refugees, minors, and those incapable of giving consent.*[2]

Such schemes are operated by various agents. Sadly, doctors have become some of them. Since they enlist patients, they have a temptation to engage in such trials.

> *Companies also recruit doctors to serve as industry-paid consultants and speakers, sponsor clinical trials where physicians are paid to enroll patients, and provide unrestricted grants to doctors, all of which to help align physicians' interests*

---

1 OECD, Health at a Glance 2011: OECD Indicators 154 (2011).

2 Guidance for Industry E6 Good Clinical Practice: Consolidated Guidance, at 1.61. As cited, Maureen Bennett & Jan Murray, Conducting Clinical Trials in the US and Abroad: Navigating the Rising Tide of Regulation and Risk 13 (2009).

with those nonprofit pharmaceutical companies and influence physicians' decision making.[1]

The same applies to biomedical researchers and laboratory technicians, where they can act as the intermediary between the pharmaceutical company and the targeted victim, of course in return for some sort of gain. On the other hand, an ambitious physician can also compromise honorable medical principles to claim a breakthrough, having testing unvetted pharmaceutical products on his patients. No external incentive is needed to commit such acts.

While financial incentives might be the most salient, at least initially, physicians also report other advantages associated with contract research: intellectual reward, increased professional status, and benefit to their patients and communities.[2]

This is to emphasize that motivations can differ and one should not imply that money is always the main motivator for committing such unlawful acts.

5.2 HEALTHCARE PERFORMERS

Physicians will be used as a convenient example here. Numerous corrupt practices engaged in by healthcare performers include informal payments and operating in the dark schemes.

---

1 T. Vian, Corruption and the Consequences for Public Health 141 (Guy Carrin ed., 2009).

2 J.A. Fisher & C.A. Kalbaugh, *United States Private-Sector Physicians and Pharmaceutical Contract Research: A Qualitative Study*, 9 PLoS Med e1001271 (2011), *available at* https://journals.plos.org/plosmedicine/article?id=10.1371/journal.pmed.1001271.

5.2.1 Informal Payments and Operating in the Dark Schemes

Studies have linked informal payments to negative impacts on the quality, efficiency and equity of health care provision.[1] Informal payments are not made solely by patients. They can be made by other players, such as device manufacturers. The following snippet from a legal case is a good illustration:

> *The Department of Justice's U.S. State Attorney for the District of New Jersey brought forth allegations against the five largest orthopedic device manufacturers for illegal kick-backs to surgeons and false claims allegations. Physicians were allegedly awarded vacations, gifts and annual (consulting) fees as high as $200,000 in return for physician endorsements of their implants or use of them in operations.*[2]

Further actions, such as unnecessary referrals to private consultations, also constitute an indirect way of perpetrating an informal payment. A physician may refer the patient to his own private practice or to another friend, who is another culpable physician. Such acts are undeniably a betrayal and disgrace to the honor of such a profession.

On a different note, not every corrupt practice is tied to money or an incentive. Sometimes things happen and are hidden, swept under the rug. This is known as "operating in the dark". The definition of operating in the dark is: "to not be informed about things that might be useful to know".[3] A doctor who has made a medical error should

---

1 M. Lewis, *Informal Payments and the Financing of Health Care in Developing and Transition Countries*, 26 Health Aff. 984 (2007).

2 W. Healy & R. Peterson, *Department of Justice Investigation of Orthopedic Industry*, 91 J. Bone & Joint Surgery Am. 1791 (2009).

3 *Be in the Dark*, Cambridge Dictionary, https://dictionary.cambridge.org/dictionary/english/be-in-the-dark (last visited Dec. 30, 2019).

be indicted, yet what happens if such incidences are either dismissed or handled in secret? A trial of malpractice will be avoided. Corruption manifests in the act of keeping medical secrets, serving the physician's private interest; in this case, preserving his professional reputation. Operating in the dark has devastating implications for the health sector. It is an act of corruption and costs lives. A patient is an easy target and a clueless victim of doctors operating in the dark.

5.3 HEALTHCARE RECIPIENTS

The category of patients will be used as a convenient example here. Corrupt practices of healthcare recipients include patients offering bribes or purposely falsifying facts.

5.3.1 Patients Offering Bribes or Purposely Falsifying Facts

To unravel this, first it is important to understand that patients are not always the victims of circumstances. At times, the patient can be in the driving seat and responsible for the behavior that constitutes corrupt actions. Such actions cause imbalance in the system and affect other patients. Here is an example:

> *a patient may bribe a doctor to obtain benefits for non-health issues, such as a health certificate to obtain a driver's license, to avoid military service or to obtain disability payments.*[1]

Another illustration that revolves around the patient as perpetrator is prescription shopping. Due to the frequency of its occurrence, this act has a nickname, "double doctoring". It is considered a drug offence in certain countries like Canada. Double doctoring is:

---

1 Savedoff & Hussmann, *supra* note X, at 10.

the practice of a patient requesting care from multiple physicians often simultaneously without making efforts to coordinate care or informing the physicians of the multiple caregivers. This usually stems from a patient's addiction to or reliance on certain prescription drugs or other medical treatment.[1]

Further corruption-related instances arising from patients' actions are mostly related to playing around with services, such as faking identity (through using the healthcare ID of another patient) in order to access healthcare services, gain exemption from healthcare costs, or obtain free prescriptions, using the IDs of patients 13 or 70 years old, in order to be eligible for such exemptions.

1 Double Doctoring, Definitions.net, https://www.definitions.net/definition/Doctor+shopping (last visited Dec. 30, 2019).

CHAPTER SIX:
HUMANITARIAN CORRUPTION

May well become the international Magna Carta of all men everywhere.
– Eleanor Roosevelt, December 1948, in Paris, France

The whole shebang is about making people's lives better. It is basically humanitarian. This final chapter is a chance to explore what can make life better, the true essence of why we fight corruption. When everything is sound and good, then corruption ceases to exist. People are able to enjoy their basic rights, beginning with the right to life. Yet this is not what is reflected around us. Wars and increasing rates of poverty and hunger persist in underdeveloped countries, whilst rage, resentment, discrimination, injustice and modern life struggles are on the rise in developing and developed countries. Both worlds have their own problems and do not seem to enjoy their full human rights.

Eleanor Roosevelt, the First Lady of the United States, was the chair of the UN Commission on Human Rights which drafted the Universal Declaration of Human Rights (UDHR), a charter which was considered to be "a guiding beacon along the way to the achievement of human rights and fundamental freedoms throughout the world".[1] It was an ambitious, brave step to eliminate all kinds of injustice. Yet what it aims to achieve seems hardly attainable when

1 Eleanor Roosevelt, "The Struggle for Human Rights". Speech Delivered in the Sorbonne, Paris (Sept. 28, 1948), *available at* https://erpapers.columbian.gwu.edu/struggle-human-rights-1948.

corruption is always lurking in the background, inevitably causing a drastic change in the narrative of the story. "Evidence has shown that all human rights can be restricted by corrupt practices, be they economic, social, cultural, civil, or political rights".[1] Tools, regulations and other mechanisms promoting the value of human welfare do exist, yet full reliance on such means will not curb corruption "until justice rolls down like water and righteousness like a mighty stream".[2] Unfortunately, many people and organisations involved in corrupt practices distort and frustrate efforts made for good.

In contrast to the previous two sections, manifestations of corruption in the humanitarian sector will be presented differently. Why? Because human rights should be enjoyed from birth and not be given by any intermediaries. The examples below will either demonstrate the promotion of human rights or their infringement. Specifically, human rights are shown to be either a goal or a target. From the perspective of humanitarian aid and charities, the promotion of human rights is a goal, while in contrast, human traffickers who contravene human rights consider human beings to be a target. For the first group, the goal is to help human beings and the target is money, while for the second, the goal is making money and the target is human beings.

6.1 HUMANITARIAN AID AND CHARITIES

In turbulent, unstable and marginalized areas of the world, people live in difficult and troubling circumstances. War, natural distress and unforeseen pandemics are some of the many factors that trigger the supply of humanitarian aid, in the form of money and supplies. The goal of humanitarian aid is to:

1 Julio Bacio-Terracino, *Corruption and Human Rights – Linking Corruption and Human Rights*, 104 Proc. Ann. Meeting Am. Soc'y Int'l L., 2010, at 243.

2 Martin Luther King Jr., "I Have a Dream". Address Delivered at the March on Washington for Jobs and Freedom (Aug. 28, 1963).

save lives, alleviate suffering and maintain human dignity during and after man-made crises and disasters caused by natural hazards, as well as to prevent and strengthen preparedness for when such situations occur.[1]

In this process, there are those who interfere and try to win the bids for supplying such aid, for the benefit of their companies. And even after the bids are granted, "the supply chain for goods and services, including fleet management, can also be subject to corrupt diversion".[2] This triggers the creation of a black market. An example from Ache in Indonesia demonstrates how assigned humanitarian aid can fail to achieve its noble aims:

More than a year after the 2004 tsunami, which left an estimated 500,000 people homeless in the Indonesian province of Aceh, many thousands of families were still living huddled in tents. Instead of settling into sturdy new homes, they were victims of the corruption which devastated the housing program of aid agencies such as Save the Children US. Given the large amounts of money and materials involved, the construction sector is especially prone to corruption – from substandard materials and workmanship, the use of incorrect measures or the theft of materials, to kickbacks for contracts and bribery or bias in land allocation. Like many agencies, Save the Children had little experience in the sector and appointed corrupt contractors who erected flimsy housing, leaving it with hundreds of homes to rebuild. "The contractors were supposed to sink foundations up to 60cm," reported the Aceh Anti-Corruption Movement in 2005, "but they'd just propped wooden stilts on

1 *Defining Humanitarian Aid*, ALNAP, https://www.alnap.org/help-library/defining-humanitarian-aid (last visited Dec. 31, 2019).

2 Transparency Int'l, Preventing Corruption in Humanitarian Operations 61 (2010).

stones and dug no foundations at all. The timber was substandard and already warping." When routine M&E revealed the shabby work, Save the Children immediately suspended construction while it investigated, issuing media statements acknowledging problems and promising to rectify them. The agency met with local communities and authorities, dismissed contractors and called in experts, establishing a multi-faceted team including experienced construction managers, architects and engineers. They worked closely with procurement staff, oversaw design development and program monitoring, and verified on-site activities. The episode also led Save the Children to strengthen anti-corruption measures beyond its Aceh construction program. It devised a specific global construction policy, and its Indonesia office established its own ombudsman committee to receive and investigate corruption allegations of any type (with a confidential whistle-blower mechanism to protect informants), and hand down sanctions, such as termination of employment and police referral. Senior staff (including the country representative and head of internal audit) gave the committee clout. By December 2007, 44 cases had been investigated, 39 of which prompted either termination or prosecution. The committee's role includes building staff capacity to prevent and detect corruption. Key to its success is the fact that both HQ and field staff know how the ombudsman system works and welcome its existence.[1]

A black market at the arrival destination of such aid is sometimes also created. Instead of delivering aid to those in need directly, aid agencies rely upon a focal point or local intermediary, who takes advantage of this position and either sells aid to those in need or decreases the level of aid.

1 *Id.* at 62.

6.2 HUMAN TRAFFICKING

Corruption is the grease that illicitly enables their movement within and across countries. Corruption is a constant companion to human trafficking and the suffering that it brings.

– Transparency International[1]

Corruption can also be described as a blind, greedy money-making machine that preys on whatever generates money, even if it is a human being, as in the case of human trafficking. Such action is facilitated by the collusion of corrupt officials with criminal gangs.[2] In simple terms, human trafficking is "the business of stealing freedom for profit".[3] This business is blind to the human qualities of its victims and pays no attention to age in its striving after profit:

> *every year, thousands of men, women and children fall into the hands of traffickers, in their own countries and abroad. Almost every country in the world is affected by trafficking, whether as a country of origin, transit or destination for victims.*[4]
> *The UN Children's Fund, UNICEF, estimates that each year 1,000 to 1,500 Guatemalan babies are trafficked to North America and Europe for adoption.*[5]

---

1 *Breaking the Chain: Corruption and Human Trafficking*, Transparency Int'l (Sept. 1, 2011), https://www.transparency.org/news/feature/breaking_the_chain_corruption_and_human_trafficking.

2 *Human Trafficking and Corruption*, OECD, https://www.oecd.org/gov/ethics/human-trafficking.htm (last visited Dec. 31, 2019).

3 *What is Human Trafficking*, Nat'l Human Trafficking Hotline, https://humantraffickinghotline.org/what-human-trafficking (last visited Dec. 31, 2019).

4 *What is Human Trafficking*, U. N. Office on Drugs and Crime, https://www.unodc.org/unodc/en/human-trafficking/what-is-human-trafficking.html (last visited Jan. 2, 2020).

5 Transparency International, *supra* note 478.

The dynamics of such phenomena and the parties involved is complicated, yet what greases and eases the wheel of its progress is corruption-related action.

Trafficking starts voluntarily, simply by recruiting victims to such schemes. Agencies, middlemen and employers shadow and trick victims into signing a vague contract, normally deceiving the victim into buying into the whole process due to poverty and other aggravating circumstances. Or, in contrast, trafficking can occur involuntarily. A common scenario is transportation, where the targeted victim uses a means of transportation with a certain arrival destination, yet once the passengers have boarded, a guaranteed arrival at the designated destination fades away! Many actors play a role in trafficking:

> *Large companies as well as local businesses can be complicit in the process by allowing the use of their transport to feed the trafficking of people in return for bribes and other illegal payments.*[1]

The case below is a typical example of the deceptive means employed in attracting victims:

> *a recruiting agency in India was looking for welders to work at a company in the United States for 10$ an hour. The agency charged each prospective worker a non-refundable 2500$ application fee. En route to the United States the workers were given contracts to sign. The contracts obligated the workers to work for the next six months for less than 3$ per hour. They could not back out because they would be sent back home. The*

1 Transparency Int'l, *Corruption and Human Trafficking* 3 (Transparency Int'l, Working Paper 03/ 2011, 2011), *available at* https://issuu.com/transparencyinternational/docs/ti-working_paper_human_trafficking_28_jun_2011?mode=window&backgroundColor=%23222222.

workers felt that they could not back out because they had invested all their savings and were already on their way to the United States. Once they arrived, they were confined to the factory grounds and the owner of the company kept their passports. Such workers were victims of a severe form of trafficking in persons. The workers were transported for the purpose of labor through the use of fraud and coercion which resulted in the workers being subject to involuntary servitude. Confiscation of the workers' passports by the employer also caused the workers to believe that they were forced to stay with the company.[1]

Trafficking cannot be sustained without corruption. It is built upon the degradation of human value. As mentioned before, it is complicated, because sometimes human beings choose to head in that direction due to hopeless and aggravating circumstances resulting from a greater web of corruption. It is all connected in one way or another. We should remember that:

Injustice anywhere is a threat to justice everywhere. We are caught in an inescapable network of mutuality, tied in a single garment of destiny. Whatever affects one directly, affects all indirectly.[2]

---

1 Hum. Smuggling &Trafficking Ctr., Fact Sheet: Distinctions Between Human Smuggling and Human Trafficking 5 (2005), *available at* https://www.justice.gov/sites/default/files/crt/legacy/2010/12/15/smuggling_trafficking_facts.pdf (see case example two).

2 Martin Luther King Jr., Letter from a Birmingham Jail (Apr. 16, 1963), *available at* https://www.africa.upenn.edu/Articles_Gen/Letter_Birmingham.html (last visited Jan. 4, 2020).

CONCLUSION AND TAKEAWAYS

This is not the end of the story. The field of anti-corruption is ever changing. There are always new, emerging practices constituting corruption, tricks that perpetrators resort to and innovative schemes to combat. Cybercrime is an example of the ever-evolving playing arena of corruption. This book has merely highlighted the most common corrupt practices in the world today.

The book began by exploring definitions of corruption and anti-corruption. History has shown us that corruption has existed throughout the ages in different eras and civilizations, and that most of its historical forms still exist today. Multiple definitions of corruption and suggested ways of viewing it or grouping together acts that constitute corruption were presented. An overview of how the world has fought corruption was given by examining the tools in place to prevent it or deal with its effects once it has happened. These tools include legal frameworks and instruments, competent authorities, initiatives and platforms. In order to make these issues relatable and relevant, the book covered specific sectors to demonstrate how corruption creeps into everything, exists everywhere and infects anything. It focused on three key areas of modern human civilization: education, health and humanitarian aid.

Key takeaways to keep in mind when approaching the issue of anti-corruption include:

- Corruption is an unwelcome guest in the view of all sensible, decent and rational human beings. It does not and will not ever resonate with them that corrupt people take what is not theirs, contributing directly or indirectly to depriving others of their rights.

- Corruption is mutant. Expect it to dress in many attires, speak in different languages and behave with unexpected behaviors. It may come in disguise, dressed as a person/organization doing good, but its effects will always be negative.
- Corruption is annoying. It irritates everything it touches and losses are incurred by those affected by it.
- Corrupt people work with stolen assets. Therefore, looking at the trail of money is key to defeating them and to restoring such assets to their rightful owners.
- Corruption happens quickly, silently and smartly. Therefore, it is vital to be bold and act fast to combat it.
- Corruption is radically progressive. Therefore, it is important to keep up to date with its latest strategies. It has reached cyber space, and from there it can reach anywhere. Constant vigilance is necessary to combat it.

Finally, it is important to realize that it is always up to the individual to keep an ethical paradigm alive in his/her actions, allowing it to dictate outcomes and audit behavior, and thus be the basis for all anti-corruption measures.